FAULTLINE

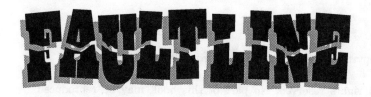

A novel by

SHEILA ORTIZ TAYLOR

The LIKE ME Lighthouse
3909 Main Street
Kansas City, MO   64111
www.LIKEMELighthouse.com

THE NAIAD PRESS, INC.
1995

Printed in the United States of America on acid-free paper
First Edition
Second printing, 1995

Cover design by Bonnie Liss (Phoenix Graphics)
Typesetting by C&H Publishing Services, Shelburne Falls, MA

Library of Congress Cataloging-in-Publication Data

Taylor, Sheila Ortiz.
    Faultline

    I. Title.
PS3570.A9544F3   813'.54   81-16922
ISBN 1-56280-108-2   AACR2

For my family, in all the best senses of that word.

SHEILA ORTIZ TAYLOR

About the Author:

I was born in Los Angeles, and my mother before me, and her mother before her. That city is in an odd way home, though I've lived in New England, the Midwest, Italy, and for the last eight years in Tallahassee, Florida, where I teach and am taught by college students, where I raise and am raised by my two daughters.

Tallahassee is in northwest Florida, sometimes called the "other" Florida. The Los Angeles I knew could as well be called the "other" Los Angeles. Not the movieland, beautiful-people Los Angeles but the one named the City of Our Lady, Queen of the Angels.

The family I knew in Los Angeles was my mother's family, thirteen children presided over by my Mexican-American grandmother, who made flour tortillas so thin you could read a book through them. Aunt Julie rolled her own cigarettes with one hand, and my Aunt Thelma could ice a cake in three strokes, standing by the conveyer belt at Van de Kamp's Bakery. My mother was a Yo-Yo painter and my father a tap dancer, lawyer, sailor, and dream maker.

Daughters of a tap dancer and a Yo-Yo painter, my sister and I were sitting ducks for the Muses, who handed her a paint set and me three yellow pencils.

—Sheila Ortiz Taylor

Portions of *Faultline* have appeared in various publications:

"A Friend of the Family" in *Focus: A Journal for Lesbians*
    September/October, 1981

"With Friends Like These" in *Lesbian Voices,* Fall, 1981

"All Things Being Equal" in *Christopher Street,* November, 1981

CONTENTS

FAULTLINE

1

A WORD FROM THE DEFENDANT

I realize that my three hundred rabbits are the most serious piece of material evidence against me. People will think only an unstable mind could not only produce but sustain that kind of absurdity. Yet absurdity is really just an event out of context, like a beached whale. So the three hundred rabbits, you might say, are really the natural outcome of a context, one so intricate that describing it might only confirm me as a lunatic. To an inattentive mind. But I am going to ask something more of you. I am asking you to keep your eye on the rabbit without forgetting the silk top hat from which the rabbit must eventually emerge. Real magic, after all, is the relationship—whether of love or of hate, I leave to you—between the rabbit and the hat.

You are wondering how I came to have three hundred rabbits. It began, of course, with two. Assuming you are not interested in the grosser mechanics of procreation, I will follow my own inclinations and assemble for you the potpourri of psychology, philosophy, sociology—adding a bouquet garni of geology, perhaps—that when properly mixed and coaxed, simmered to a roux will account for what you are pleased to call this fact of the three hundred rabbits.

I was born on the San Andreas Fault. Naturally I am not alone in this distinction, but I believe we choose our own metaphors, not the other way around. These millions born along the fault do not accept that fact, as I do, in all its metaphoric glory. Which is not to conclude they are witless; their tastes for metaphor simply swim in other currents. And after all, I am a poet.

Picture, if you will, a tiny child standing next to her mother's knee, watching with wonder as the water in the toilet bowl swirls and eddies before her wondering eyes. Emblem of change! Those tumultuous waters were but minute symptoms of the larger stirrings beneath our feet, rumblings and burblings that might someday crack the earth, sliding Santa Monica and the Pacific Palisades into the sea like so many biscuits off the cookie sheet of existence.

My mother's calm attitude as we gazed together into the toilet can be attributed to her Indian blood. If she had felt free to explain the tremor as the Goddess, restless on her sleeping mat, I might not have ended up with those three hundred rabbits. Tamed as she was, she gave the usual dose of one part science mixed with three parts offhand ignorance. Whether it was the science or the ignorance that did it, that experience left me with a faultline of cold fear running through a basic Indian friendliness toward tremors of the earth. I never told you this would be simple.

To continue: if sanity consists of fear melted down and poured into socially useful shapes, I should say my maternal instincts—along with whatever shadowy biological sources you may care to mention—spring directly from this childhood fear that the earth may suddenly split open, devouring greater Los Angeles in a single bite.

So at the exact moment serious-minded adults began to organize their arguments against overpopulation, I conceived the idea that underpopulation was the real threat. Therefore by the age of eight I had laid my plans. I would have six children and drive them in a yellow school bus, a prophecy which like many before it was greeted with laughter and some contempt, only to become a problem of high seriousness to everybody later.

Now that I have my yellow bus of children you begin to question my ability to drive. Which explains your preoccupation with the three hundred rabbits. To me it's saner having three hundred rabbits than obsessing over someone else's having three hundred rabbits.

Anyway, the six children were simply my answer to the San Andreas Fault, along which I have camped so long we two are like old and quarrelsome lovers.

In all my reveries of the busload of children, I confess, the image of a man never flickered. Not that your conditioning had no effect on me. Anyone married, as I was, for twelve long years must be credited with having given heterosexuality a spirited try. Left to my own devices, I would never have married anybody for the single reason that he resembled William Holden. And I am sure if the song called "When I Fall in Love, It Will Be Forever" hadn't been etched into my brain by processes verging on sleep teaching, I might have been happily divorced years ago.

No, I did not spring from my mother's loins a lesbian, though I have met in the past year or two several promising young women who believe they did. Instead I tap-danced out of my mother's womb flanked by Shirley Temple and Ginger Rogers, watching apprehensively yet faithfully out of the corner of my eye for the appearance of Captain January or Fred Astaire, whichever occurred first. But it was William Holden, as I have said before.

His name was Malthus. Whitney Malthus, actually, though everybody— including his own mother—called him Malthus, an ominous enough sign, if I had been looking for signs.

We met by chance at the Griffith Park Planetarium one balmy evening in early summer. He explained to me rather tediously the earth's rotation on its axis. Malthus is one of those people determined to know how everything works and equally determined that you will hear him explain it. At length.

I had been sitting on a bannister watching the giant pendulum below swinging back and forth, knocking down wooden pins for upwards of an hour without troubling myself or anybody else for an explanation. Malthus must have seen uncritical appreciation written all over my face, an expression that drives him mad. At the time I had no idea how to deal with people determined to deliver a forty-minute lecture on the rotation of the earth on its axis. Now I would pretend I was a deaf-mute, or yell rape. Probably the latter.

At the time, though, I admired people whose minds organized experience into forty-minute waves that washed over their listeners. Why? Let me explain.

In freshman history I had learned about the tabula rasa, turning poor Locke's slate into a five-and-dime cardboard model that you wrote on with a stylus, flicking up the cellophane overlay to erase everything instantly. For years I believed that every night, while I slept, some imp flicked up the cellophane of the day's experience, and every morning I had to start over again the terrible labor of covering that slate with vital statistics. This was in the days when I confused facts with knowledge.

My own mind, I was convinced, couldn't lay claim to a single fact.

When I was a kid I used to try to memorize the facts on Double Bubble wrappers. My plan was to memorize one fact a day for a year. Three hundred and sixty-five facts seemed like enough to get one through life. Things went all right until the fourth fact: "The average man eats three times as much lettuce now as he did in 1919."

Innocent enough on the surface, the fact was like a nest of black widow spiders just hatching out. Why the sudden attraction to lettuce? Has the average woman also increased her lettuce consumption? Why does *average* mean? These questions were confusing enough, but what really threw me was the thought that with every passing year my fourth fact would be less valid. Granted that in 1950 the average man ate three times as much lettuce as he did in 1919, by 1960 he might be eating four or even five times as much! Weren't facts supposed to hold still?

What did I know? I was an English major.

When I met Malthus I was an English major out of a job because once you get your B.A., logically speaking you can't keep on being an English major, but there seems nothing in particular you can be instead. So I was an English major on the skids, loitering about the planetarium, just days after that strange ceremony at UCLA where there are so many graduates they don't mention anybody's name, but just nod in your general direction when it's time for you to flip your tassel from the left side of the mortarboard to the right. Or is it from the right to the left?

See what I mean? It's that lingering worry about facts. Maybe you can see now why Malthus, with his facts about celestial bodies, made such inroads on my normally sceptical self. Somewhere in me lurked the fear—not unrelated to my feelings about earthquakes—that if I, Arden Benbow, did not know how the earth turned on its axis, it might stop. Out of spite.

So while Malthus was giving his forty-minute special on rotation, in my mind a battle raged silently. Part of me, maybe it was the poet part or the Indian part, wanted to tweak his nose and dance around him whooping. The other part—whose firm, still voice had the power to silence twenty braves on a peyote trip—stepped forward, adjusted her white gloves, and suggested it might be prudent in a person with a mind like a colander to attach herself to a promising young man (who looked like William Holden) with a mind like an electric can opener.

Now this unattractive person in the white gloves, dressed like an Avon lady, exists in any woman who did not spring from her mother's loins as a fully constituted lesbian. Before her my Indian self cowered and—so as to have some say in the matter—resigned herself to an unreasoning love for the part of Malthus that looked like William Holden, trying obstinately for twelve long years to ignore the part of Malthus that *would* explain the earth's rotation on its axis, or Cartesian dualism, or the Bloodless Revolution, or continental drift, or the gold standard, or whatever else would not let him be.

When I first met him that auspicious August in 1959 he was just beginning graduate school, working on a master's degree in city planning, a happy choice in his case. He was fascinated, he said, that nature should be so orderly while society was so sloppy. He thought society might be tidied up a bit, and that if you had ample parking, convenience markets, community centers, and nightly bingo, crime and suicide might well disappear. If the earth had an axis then so might society. And if it didn't, then you could always build it one out of high-impact plastic. Malthus is successful in his work.

You are quietly leaping to conclusions. I can hear the soft pad of your feet as you drop down and position yourself for the next leap, like kids in an after-school ballet class. I didn't become a lesbian because Malthus is sexually unsatisfying.

It is true that Malthus brought to bear on sex a rather scholarly sense of excitement. Probably he read illustrated books during our engagement. He had the delicacy not to discuss them, or in fact ever to mention sex except in its general anatomical sense. Just before our marriage he gave me a copy of *Women's Medical Problems,* showing some sensitivity toward what he called my "virgin state." It was unclear from the book whether marriage was the cause or the cure. Very clear was the implication that either Malthus or the author, or both, believed womanhood was all by itself already a medical problem.

On our honeymoon he brought a tube of KY Jelly.

You see, I am trying to be fair with Malthus. Partly that is because my moon is in Libra, and partly it is because I have a poet's concern for truth, and partly it is because I am so angry with him I would like to cut out his liver and roast it.

2

A FORTY-MINUTE LECTURE

Any thinking person will agree that the term *lesbian mother* is oxymoronic. The oxymoron is a figure of speech in which the adjective modifying a noun contradicts the essence of the noun it modifies; as in, *burning snow*. Snow, you will agree, is cold, and to modify the noun *snow* with the descriptive quality *burning* outrages our sense of logic. Do you follow?

Now the concept of *mother* implies cohesiveness in the social tissue. Mothers raise offspring to adapt to their environment and in turn to work for its preservation and refinement. Mothers, true mothers, are gentle, self-sacrificing, living for the good of their families.

What is a lesbian? A social deviate. Even, we might say, an unwitting social enemy. By her very existence she defies and discredits the family, inverting the natural order of things, asserting her own ego at the expense of organized society.

The term *lesbian mother,* then, simply makes no sense. Granted, a woman who is a lesbian may have a child. She is, we may say, a biological mother. But she will lack the tenderest instincts of a real, or we might say, of a social mother, and will quite simply lack both the ability and the desire to make her own needs subservient to those of the child and his environment.

Of course, Arden does not agree with me and uses her poetic vagaries to dismiss what she cannot refute. On one occasion she actually threw an umbrella stand through the patio door, then turned to me and said, "You probably don't believe in unicorns, either."

Arden sometimes pretends I have no understanding of the figurative. She treats me as if I have no feelings.

It isn't that I want to punish her. She did not intend to humiliate me. She cannot help being ill. But it would be very wrong in me to allow my feelings to override my reason. After all, as a city planner I believe I have some understanding of family structure and social cohesion. Children learn through emulation. I have my boys to think of. Not that I'm what you would call a male chauvinist. Still, there are differences between men and women, say what you will. And vive la différence! Right?

Understand I have nothing against homosexuals. Certainly they have enough misfortune in their lives without our mockery. Tormented creatures! But how could I permit my sons—and even my daughters—to be exposed and possibly recruited into the ranks of the socially maimed? What kind of life could that be? What father could stand by and watch his innocent children tottering unguided toward an abyss?

Now if Arden were in love with some other man—a lawyer, or a doctor, or even a dentist—I would never consider taking these steps to win custody of the children. For children—I would say, speaking in a professional capacity—belong with their mother. The mother is the cornerstone of the American family. Therefore, it is precisely and exclusively on this conviction, viz., that lesbianism and motherhood are at war, on which I rest my case.

3

JUST FOR THE RECORD

I'm Arden Benbow's feed man. You might say all this ruckus started with me. You see, she bought a baby rabbit from me for her next to oldest kid, Jamie. The one with her front teeth out? Well, that one run away—the rabbit, I mean—and they looked all over hell-and-gone. No rabbit. So Arden comes back a couple of days later and buys another one. For Jamie, you know. Because the other one run away. Like I told you.

Then, sure as I'm standing here, they find the first one. Dog digs it up out of its warren. Now they got two.

Well, you know what that means, but not Miss Benbow. Not that she's ignorant. No sir. Smart as a bird dog. But there's things she just don't think about and that was sure one of them.

There's another thing you ought to know too. About rabbits. Never saw the like. See, I'm from Iowa. Olwang? And we used to raise rabbits on the farm, of course. And they multiplied like rabbits. Ha!

But here in San Fernando Valley, why, hell, there ain't nothing like it for sheer productivity. Got something to do with those tremors. You see, we're on top of one of them cracks. Not that you can see it. But those scientists know it's there. And so do those rabbits, too, you can bet. It just sets them shivering and a-jumping and making babies till hell won't have it.

So it really ain't Miss Benbow's fault, her having them three hundred rabbits and all. It might be mine, and it might be that there crack through

9

the valley, but I just don't see how it's hers and how you mean to take those kids away from her. She's smart as a bird dog about everything besides rabbits and she pays her feed bill real regular. There's not many you can say that about these days and that's a fact.

4

A FRIEND OF THE FAMILY

When I got to Arden's house in the late afternoon she was sitting on the back steps having a drink with her feed man. It was one of those hot July afternoons in the San Fernando Valley, when you just can't stay inside. There were packages of hot dogs out on the redwood table, and Kip, the oldest, was starting a fire in the barbecue by rubbing two sticks together.

At least once a week I stop in to see Arden and the kids, since the divorce. It seems like in every divorce someone gets custody of the friends, and in this case it was Malthus. Not that people didn't like Arden. It was two things, I guess. One was Arden's always being a little different. Well, okay, very different. And the other was the rather unusual nature of the split. It would have been bad enough if Arden had fallen in love with one of Malthus's colleagues, but Arden fell in love with a colleague's wife. See what I mean?

The reason I know all this is I'm one of Malthus's colleagues. No, it wasn't my wife. Everybody says I would feel differently if it was, but I'm not sure that's true.

Because, you see, I love Arden. I told her so one night at a party. We all had a little too much fish house punch. She and I walked into the back yard, feeling companionable, and stopped at a fence. I remember feeling a strange sense of energy and then saying, "I love you, Arden." She thanked me. We stood there a while, looking at some horses on the other side of the fence. I think they were asleep. Then we went back into the house.

This was not a sexual encounter, though it had something to do with sex. Or sexuality. Mostly it was a kind of generous, disembodied movement from me to her, and back again. It was not the beginning of anything, but was more like the middle.

So I like to think that out of this feeling, if it had been my wife, I would have behaved well.

Malthus did not. Usually behaving well is Malthus's strongest suit. There is a clean, generous look about him that most people find disarming. They want to elect him to some post. Of course, there is more to him than that, as we were to find out, those of us who keep a scorecard. But there can be no doubt that he was angry in a dangerous kind of way, that he had lost his wife in an unfair competition (Malthus sees life in those terms), that people would laugh at him, that his career would be ruined.

Malthus believed he had a career, whereas I am the kind of person who does not know what that means. I know what having a job means, or what having measles means, or even what having a boring time means. But I do not know what having a career means. For Malthus, a career was as real as his living room furniture, and he fully believed he was being robbed of his.

On this particular afternoon Arden and I still did not know about Malthus's plans for a custody dispute. That came later. It was just one afternoon in a string of afternoons. Except that something happened. I can't tell you exactly what it meant, only what it was, and that it belongs here somehow.

Well, I got myself a beer from the refrigerator, and joined Arden and her feed man on the back steps. I knew Ben Griffin pretty well, because our rounds to Arden's house would sometimes overlap. This is before the main warren caved in, when Arden had something like five hundred rabbits.

It started, if I remember correctly, with two. There was a small barn in the back yard, with chicken wire nailed across the front and a dirt floor. Through the chicken wire you could see only a few rabbits at a time, but underneath their feet in miles of uncharted tunnels radiating out from the barn lived Ben Griffin's unseen but vigorous customers.

Like many yards in the Valley, Arden's was large—half an acre, at least. Up close to the house was a strip of lawn, beaten down by the traffic of dogs and children from the yard into the house and back. Beyond the lawn were winding dirt paths, looping around pine trees: an ideal place for cowboys and Indians. And the whole was enclosed with Cyclone fencing.

To the east was the neighboring house, similar, though in better repair than Arden's, and to the west was an abandoned chicken ranch, a gully, and not much else. They lived on a dead-end street. There was an appealing kind of quiet to it, though they lived just five minutes from the Golden State Freeway and the Budweiser Brewery, from which an occasional condor would wander in, and once a pink flamingo.

Griff was weaving some kind of yarn about when he used to work for the railroads, and Arden kept gently interrupting to mention her grandmother—an Indian princess, or something—and Kip kept on rubbing his two sticks together to get the barbecue lit. Bruce, their black and brown and otherwise indescribable dog, was dozing on a pile of kindling.

Suddenly Bruce, who seldom looked alert, did. He jumped quivering to his feet, ears pricked, tail straight out, as if obeying some obscure and distant ancestor. Arden was on her feet the next instant, looking every inch the Indian she claimed to be. When Bruce broke into a run, she was right behind him, leaving Griff and me on the porch thinking they had both gone crazy. Then Kip got the message, threw down his sticks, and took out after his mother. The next thing we knew the whole house had emptied of kids, running in file behind their brother.

For a moment the whole train of them disappeared. Then we saw it: the rabbit. Looking like fear itself, he rounded the nearest pine, a breath ahead of Bruce, with Arden just behind, yelling incoherently to the dog, and Kip behind her, then the whole string of them: Jamie, Hillary, Arthur, Max, and even the baby, Ellen. Griff jumped up and fell into line behind the baby, but I decided to double around the opposite way.

It was already stifling, and now the air was choked with dust. I was rounding my third pine, and though I couldn't see for the dust and shrubs, I could hear that express of animals and people pounding toward me. The rabbit had gained a little on everybody, so when I first saw him, he seemed alone.

He was a big one, and white, with splashes of black that made him look like he was moving even faster than he was. Just as I flung out my hands, he broke and ran in a third direction, and was—without losing momentum—running full tilt toward the chain link fence at the western boundary.

I stopped dead, and Arden almost knocked me down, with the kids sliding in behind her, then Griff. We all froze together, just watching that rabbit hurtling along, aimed straight at that fence and certain oblivion. Nobody looked away, and nobody made a move, and next thing we knew that rabbit ran *through* the fence, never hesitating, and was gone.

"Belief," said Arden.

"Yes," I said.

5

THREE HUNDRED OLD ENGLISH SHEEPDOGS

Now I just love rabbit, and that's how I met Arden Benbow. I love rabbit just about the best of anything I ever did sink my pearlies into. I love rabbit so much I have a reputation for it.

So one day I get this here call from my old friend Griff. Jim, he says, old Jim, I do believe I can put my hands on some prime rabbit for you, if you can just meet the price. Well, I says, Griff, old buddy, you know how I do love rabbit. What're they asking? They're free, Jim! he says right out. Must be a catch to it, I says, kind of suspicious-like, pretending, really. I know old Griff ain't gonna see Big Jim took. Kind of sly-like he says, Well, yes, Big Jim, there might be one little tiny catch to it. And I can hear him laughing fit to kill. Trying to muffle the sound, you know.

But I go along with it because next to rabbit, I love Ben Griffin best thing in this world. So he gives me an address where I'm to meet him next Saturday afternoon, and I'm to bring my truck, and ask for Arden Benbow. Well, I'm looking forward to Saturday, on account of mostly I live a quiet kind of life, off in the Malibu Hills. I used to have a girl, Winnifred. Winnifred Hooper. Used to be the postmistress over to Topanga Canyon. But she run off. Can't fault her for that. Got tired of waiting, I guess. Run off three years ago come May with a used car salesman from Chula Vista.

I'm kind of a loner. Griff and Winnifred are the only friends I got, and since Winny run off three years ago (come May), that just leaves old Griff.

Don't see much of him, hardly. I live with dogs. Old English sheepdogs. Make fine pets. Fine watchdogs, too.

Oh, maybe you didn't know, I'm Muncey from Muncey's Old English Sheepdog Farms. You might of heard about me. My dogs got a reputation. Actually there isn't but one Muncey farm, but I call it "farms" to throw a little class into it. But it's a pretty big spread. Upwards of three hundred dogs. You can't beat it for nights, up here. Just after sunset it gets real quiet. Then old Josh, the daddy of them all, lifts up that head and lets out six or seven good ones. Next thing you know there's a regular hallelujah chorus out here under the stars. Specially when the moon's full and bright. They just sing it out, they do. Bless 'em. Damned good company. Good watchdogs, too.

Anyway, Saturday come, and after dinner I get into the pickup and head for the Valley, where I know old Griff has got up something fine.

It's a dead-end street I'm looking for, and I get lost a couple of times, till I see this bunch of kids selling lemonade on a street corner. Must of been half a dozen of 'em. So I pull up and buy a glass—by this time it's hot as a pistol, maybe a hundred—and wave the oldest kid over.

"What's your name, kid?" I ask him.

"Copernicus," he says.

They're all snickering something fierce by now, so I figure he's putting me on. "Well, Copernicus, old boy," I says, "can you tell me where Tilden Street is at?"

Now they are laughing fit to bust because I'm on the corner of Hearst and Tilden with egg on my face. This other kid, a girl, points up at the signpost, and shoots me the biggest snaggletooth smile. Jamie, she tells me her name is, and she asks me who I'm looking for.

"Arden Benbow," I tell her.

"Well, come on, then," she tells me.

Next thing I know the whole kit and caboodle, along with their dog, pile into the back of the truck, with this Jamie hanging off the running board, ready to direct.

"Listen, kid," I tell her, "your mother wouldn't like this. How do you know I'm not some kind of maniac?"

"Are you?" she asks me, pulling a long face.

"No," I says, "I ain't."

"That's what I thought," she says brightening up again and motioning me ahead.

After a couple of blocks we pull into the gravel drive, smack at the end of the street. There's flowers in the yard, and lots of shade, and an old house kind of falling down in places but nice anyway, real nice.

Griff isn't here yet, and I'm sitting in the truck not knowing what to do, and these kids jumping up and down, jiggling the living daylights out of me, when through the screen door comes this lady. She looks to be somewhere around thirty or so—hard to say—in Indian braids with a kerchief tied around her forehead. Got on an undershirt kind of thing with colors looking like they're melting on her, blue jeans, and moccasins. I figure she is some kind of a nut. I figure Griff has gone one too far this time.

Well, she comes over to the truck, puts her hand out for a shake, gives me a big smile kind of like her kid's, and says she's real glad to see me and how I must be Mr. Muncey about who she's heard lots.

"You the lady with the rabbit?" I ask her.

"Rabbits," she corrects me. Then she kind of waves her hand over her eyes, like she's driving off a fly, and invites me in. But just then Griff pulls up in his feed truck and the fun is about to start.

It seems this lady's got upwards of four hundred rabbit, and it's all she can do to feed them six kids, let alone the rabbit. Now anybody with half a brain could get at both these problems with one swipe. I don't mean Miss Benbow was an ace short. It's just that to her, rabbits was rabbits, and to me they was rabbit. Stewed, baked, roasted, pan fried, poached, broiled, barbecued—any way at all. Just let me at 'em!

Not that I lied to her. I told her flat out I liked rabbit, again, just to make sure, before we got too far into the thing. And she made that little brushing away motion again with her hand, and I took it to signify that she got my meaning and could see my point, but that it just wasn't her way while it might be others'.

So now we made a plan, because the catch I knew there must be in this deal was that the rabbit was loose in a dirt-floored barn, which meant, of course, they was to hell and gone all over half an acre of ground. But all the holes was in the barn. Nothing to do but sit in that dusty, sweaty shack waiting for one to show, and then going for that loose skin round the back of the neck, like a mother cat goes for her kitten.

Well, we kept at it for a couple of hours. Sitting and jumping, grabbing and sprawling, falling in the dirt, empty-handed often as not. When we got one we'd pass it through the barn door, real quiet, to one of the kids, then off to the truck it would go, and into one of the cages old Griff had brought along.

Naturally the kids didn't catch the difference between rabbits and rabbit, being that the oldest one was only ten or so. I felt kinda bad about that. Wasn't much else to do, though, them being so strapped for cash and all, and the population growing every time you blew your nose.

Anyway, after two hours of this we had about sixty rabbit, according to the kids. That wasn't nearly enough, you can bet. Must of been upwards of three hundred more down in them warrens and by then they had the word about what was happening at home plate. Wasn't a chance in hell we'd catch more than two or three if we sat there all night.

Figuring at least a hundred and fifty down them holes was females, in six weeks Arden Benbow was going to have nine hundred rabbit, maybe a cool thousand. There just wasn't any stopping it. I felt real bad for her. Finally the three of us went inside, washed up at the kitchen sink, and had the leftover lemonade.

Then Griff said he had to go make deliveries. I could tell he felt bad too. That lady had a way of growing on you. Know what I mean? She stuck to things. So I wanted to cheer her up and help her find a way out of this mess, if I could.

"You know, Miss Benbow," I said, kind of casual, as we walked to the truckload of rabbit, "I just never had any luck raising rabbit." She smiled like I was pulling her leg. "No, I mean it. They just won't breed for me."

Now the smile melted into something else. That one got her, you can believe.

"Why do you think that is, Jim?" she asks me.

"Well, Miss Benbow, it's the dogs. Rabbit won't breed when dogs bark. That's a plain fact. I got three hundred Old English sheepdogs barking night and day. Rabbit won't touch each other on a bet."

Then I blow my nose kind of thoughtful. "Listen, Miss Benbow, I could sell you a real nice bitch. Let you have her for cost. You could breed her and by and by get you a nice little income on the side."

For just a minute there she looked like she was about to go for it. Then she pulled up like she was getting herself in hand, smiled in a tired kind of way, thanked me for all my help, and walked back into the house, whacking the dust off her britches in slow clouds.

She could of been an A-1 dog breeder, and no mistake.

6

DO YOU HAVE PRINCE ALBERT IN A CAN?

You probably don't know this, but vets' offices get as many crank calls as pizza parlors. Bad enough to be a receptionist, but this is like overtime and no extra pay. People thinking they're cute. Honestly!

So how am I supposed to know this is on the up and up? She doesn't even say hello. All she says is, "Do you have birth control pills for rabbits?"

Well, I don't fall for it. You know what I mean? Best way to deal with this type of call is to pretend it's serious. That's the first step. If that doesn't do it, next step is you throw the joke back at them. Simplest of all is to tell them where to put it, but Doctor Packer doesn't like that a bit. Besides, step one usually works.

So I say to her, "We don't have birth control pills for rabbits."

"What do people do about rabbits?" she asks.

"We could neuter them," I suggest.

"Three hundred rabbits?" she explodes.

"Well . . . maybe we could offer you group rates," I say, moving on to step two and quietly hanging up the phone.

7

ALL THINGS BEING EQUAL

I'm Wilson Topaz, student of the dance.

Actually I'm a student of a lot more than that. I watch. I'm taking notes. Nothing escapes me.

Scared you, didn't I? You're not scared because I'm six foot three in my stocking feet. You're scared because I'm black, gay, and six foot three in my stocking feet. Right? See, I'm watching.

So you want to know about Arden Benbow. Well, I went to work for Arden right after my little altercation with the University of California. It was about money. They made out it was over a point of honor, but it was really over money, of course. But that's another story.

All summer I had worked at the Hollywood Bowl, sometimes dancing, sometimes hawking opera glasses. Mostly it was opera glasses. Oh, I have talent. It isn't that. But I tend to stand out in a line of gents in tuxedos, or anywhere else, for that matter. The last choreographer I worked with said I was larger than life. I take that as a compliment.

So I was out of work, the university had declined my loan, as I have said, and I was a month behind in my rent. It looked like my mother's worst fears were about to be realized.

Everybody's mother has a worst fear for her child. I guess mothers worry that their daughters will become whores and that their sons will be gay. Or maybe it's fathers who worry about this last possibility. Anyway, since I had already explored and embraced that worst fear, my mother moved along to the next available worst fear, that I would become a drag queen. Actually I haven't got the mentality of a drag queen, but she doesn't understand that. And because any fear is real to the person that's got it, I try to take hers seriously. You know? So she was the other reason I had to find work in a hurry.

But there just wasn't much work around. Especially not for someone black, six foot three in his stocking feet, with an aversion to violence. Without this last qualification, I could have had plenty of work.

Well, one morning on my way to ballet, I passed the bulletin board next to the drinking fountain and something caught my eye, a blue index card, carefully lettered, saying

LESBIAN MOTHER

needs child care in own home.
Small salary, board, private
room. Equal opportunity
employer.

and then her phone number. There was a lot there to mull around. That night I gave her a call.

"Hello," says a kid's voice. Then there are sounds of scuffling and another voice off in the distance asking who is it.

"Who is this?" asks the first voice.

"Wilson Topaz."

"It's Joan Baez," screams the kid's voice to the voice off in the distance.

"Listen, kid," I say, getting pissed, "do I sound like Joan Baez?"

"What?" says the kid. Then the receiver hits the floor, and I am on the point of hanging up, when the voice of reason asks can it help me. I don't need to tell you about Arden Benbow's voice, if you've heard it. Like Ben Gay on a sore muscle. It's the muse in tails.

"Hello," I say, "are you the lesbian mother?" Just testing her, you see. I really knew she was, on account of her voice. It made you think of unicorns in moonlight.

"Yes it is," she answers, so cool, like I had asked if she was Golda Meir, and she was. I figure she has not been around much.

"I saw your ad."

"Yes, I know." There is barking in the background, and scuffing sounds, then the lady issuing directives with her hand over the receiver. Then, "Look, Mr. . . . ."

"Wilson, Topaz Wilson."

"Mr. Wilson. It would be best if you came out here—we live in the Valley—for an interview. Can you do that tomorrow? Late afternoon?"

By now I was beginning to get cold feet. How did I know I even liked children? I had always liked them in the past, but people took them away when I got tired of them. There would be none of that in this situation. When I am panicked my subconscious floods my conscious, like high tide into the streets of Venice, and I am likely to say anything.

"You should know that I'm a drag queen."

There was a pause, one of those brief ones that feels long, and an undertone of barks, laughs, and squeals. Then she says, "Well, Mr. Wilson, I see no reason why we can't arrange your hours around your job schedule."

That pretty much did it. If she was willing to accept me in the costume of my mother's worst fantasy, then I was willing to accept the yelling and barking. At least on a trial basis.

What you are really interested in is how Arden and I came to be arrested. I'm coming to that. By your impatience I can tell you are losing your fear of me. You begin to see me as life size. Why can't you see me as life size in a chorus line at the Hollywood Bowl?

It all depends on what you're looking for, in art or in life. If you've got a dozen studs up there, dancing in tuxedos, well you want them all to look alike. Then you shift around on your ass, bored. You think symmetry and harmony are the same thing, when they can't even get it on, mostly. But symmetry is a ten-dollar whore and you want her. That makes you a bad audience. And it puts me out of work.

Which brings me back to my story. It was a pretty typical Sunday evening, early evening. I had been working for Arden nearly four months, and had left off pretending I was doing drag shows. Usually I went out tricking Friday and Saturday nights, but otherwise I was either rehearsing at the university or helping out at home. Not that the adjustment was easy. There was six of them, after all, ranging in ages from three to ten, and in disposition from A to Zed. That was Arden's little surprise.

Work agreements are kind of like weddings. Both people have collections of mysterious objects they judge unnecessary at the ceremony, but bring along on the honeymoon. By telling Arden I was a drag queen, I flatter myself I had prepared her for anything. But there was the matter of my blackness, my height, and even my sex that some might have found objectionable. Arden's surprises included, as I have said, the six kids, together with a dog, a lover, three hundred rabbits, debts, and an old house in an advanced state of decay. Not to mention that son-of-a-bitch ex-husband, skulking around like Satan's meter-reader.

Well, since it was Sunday, we had all had a strong dose of Malthus. In his case "visitation" was exactly the word. You wanted to draw a circle around yourself to ward off evil spirits. When he was in the house you kept checking him in mirrors to make sure he cast a reflection.

So after these Sundays, we all tended to spread ourselves out even more than usual. Big Jim Muncey was here, lying under the kitchen sink fixing a leaky pipe, Earl—a friend of the family—was playing chess with Jamie on half the kitchen table, while on the other, her brother Kip was stinking up the house with his chemistry set. Hillary was running around in her pajamas, trying to make Jim's sheepdog eat a peanut butter sand-wich. Arthur was playing the coronet, while Alice, Arden's lover, counted time. Arden and I were bathing the last two, Max and Ellen.

Now you can see all this as chaos or process, depending on your point of view. But it had all somehow come out of Arden Benbow, and I was determined to get used to it, somehow. I started by painting my room chalk white and making it off limits. Next night I found a rubber taran-tula in my bed. That was when I installed the deadbolt lock. I gave Arden a key, and she hid out there sometimes when the process started to bubble backwards toward chaos.

Finally Jim got the plumbing right, washed up in the kitchen sink, scrubbed the peanut butter out of his dog's hair, and said goodnight. Then Jamie beat Earl at chess, so we were in a fair way to get them to bed, and have a quiet grown-up evening. I thought.

Of course the final push was always the hardest. There were those end-less glasses of water, gum in the hair, and last-minute pisses. The kids had two bedrooms, three to a room, in bunkbeds stacked up like Dagwood sandwiches. Copernicus—named by that asshole Malthus—headed up the boys' room, and Jamie, who was ten, was in charge of the girls'. That kind of blend between autocracy and democracy worked mostly, but I did sometimes think a heavy hand now and then would have been more to the point.

Anyway, they were in bed, if not asleep. Earl went into the kitchen to make a batch of his strange blender drinks. He always pretended his recipes came out of magazines, but we all knew he was experimenting on us. Alice and Arden were sitting on the old couch, cozying up to each other, so I built them a fire, and went in to watch old Earl and his blender wizardry.

It was some kind of green mess, into which he had just dropped one of the rawest eggs I have ever seen. Quickly he whirred it up, hoping I wouldn't notice. Next the rum went in, light then dark. Earl kept the liquor cabinet stocked, as well as beer in the refrigerator. Mostly he drank the beer, but it was nice of him anyway. He spent a lot of time at our house. I think he found all the noise and rioting around peaceful.

He invited me to taste the green froth, passing me the blenderful, and then he drank some too. It needed something. We tried some triple sec and a shade more rum. It tasted better, but still wasn't quite right. A dash of drambuie and the whole thing turned purple. More rum, more tastes. In the living room the fire had gone out silently. I stoked it discreetly. Then back in the kitchen, a dash of bitters and a jigger of rum. Earl confessed he played the oboe in high school. We threw in some crushed ice and a little kahlua, and carried the pitcher into the living room, smiling like conspirators.

It was over that blender of mystery cocktail that we formulated Operation Bunnylift. You see, Arden had three hundred rabbits. And not much income. Malthus talked big, but kicked in a pittance for child support, considering there were six kids and Arden was in school. She had a fellowship, one high on prestige and low on currency. Alice, before all the divorces, had been promising as a provider. Then she got the fever for change, quit her job, and in her forties started graduate school. At night she sometimes did free-lance technical writing. When she could get it. So we were a houseful of indigent geniuses, surrounded by an army of bunnies whose jaws never stopped working. Not even at night.

Operation Bunnylift, as I remember, was Alice's idea initially. She said they should be "relocated," like the Japanese in California during the war. Arden knew of a gully in Topanga Canyon, not far from Big Jim's sheepdog ranch, where there was a stream and plenty of grass. We began to plan.

Somebody had to stay with the kids. Alice volunteered because she had some work to do anyway. Arden was supposed to have a sonnet written by 10 A.M. but was too caught up to resist. She had taken it into her head that there should be a motorcycle escort, that Earl and I should drive the rabbits in the school bus, and she would lead on her Harley Davidson. Besides, she said, things came to her when she rode at night.

It took us a good hour, scrambling around in the dark in that falling-down barn, to get a respectable supply of bunnies. I guess we got about thirty into cages. Not even a dent, but we decided Bunnylift would happen in stages, like Corregidor.

Alice and Earl and I arranged the cages down the middle aisle of their old school bus, while Arden disconnected the sidecar from the motorcycle. We told her to leave it on, but by then she was marching to her own goddamned drummer. The sidecar had to come off. And then nothing would do but she had to put on her jodhpurs and boots. While she was at it, she slipped into a white silk blouse and a smart midnight-blue leather jacket with fifteen zippers, and tied a flowing scarf around her neck. This was at the height of her Amelia Earhart phase.

Finally we were ready, and the convoy moved out some time around midnight, with Alice whirling the flashlight, directing us down the driveway and into the street.

After all the noise and running around, it was still and quiet out on the streets, like everybody had gone to bed and left us to run the world. We started up the freeway ramp, and I could see Earl in the bars of green light, hunched over the giant wheel, his hand on the gearshift, looking a little like Art Carney. I started to laugh. First he looked at me, maybe a little annoyed. Then he started to laugh, and—as if she heard us—Arden turned her head for a split second in our direction and shot us this smile that lit up the whole Valley.

Actually we were not drunk by this time. Instead there were little time-released capsules of excitement going off inside us. The rabbits must have felt it too. When I turned around to look at them, they were nuzzling and climbing over each other, biting necks, and otherwise inviting population explosion. So I thought I'd put on a tape to quiet them. Alice was an opera buff and had rigged up two oversize speakers at the back of the bus. I thumbed through the tapes but it was hard to know what a bunny would appreciate. Somehow I thought Wagner would be a big mistake.

Finally I decided they wanted something rich, something mellow, a blue sound to wind around the excitement. I put on Ellington's "Satin Doll." I choreographed it. I was Fred Astaire in a white tuxedo. Behind me, a sea of ears swayed in time and sympathy. I imagined them in tiny tuxedos, two lines of fifteen bunnies, one on each side of me. They carried canes with pearl handles. I was no longer Fred Astaire, but Topaz Wilson, six foot three in his stocking feet, dancing his heart out with thirty tapping bunnies. It was beautiful.

We began to wind into the hills, Arden leading, with her silk scarf snapping behind, murmuring her sonnet into the night. I had Ella Fitzgerald on now, and the ears were swaying dreamily. But beyond the ears, I picked up on a sight not so dreamy. Headlights following at a discreet distance, taking every turn we made.

Now black people tend toward paranoia, and gay people the same. Me, I'm double jeopardy. Those headlights meant trouble. Those headlights meant somebody had a library book that was overdue.

I pointed them out to Earl and he told me I was paranoid. Any white, heterosexual, employed, necktie-wearing stud in his late forties can afford such confidence. Even the bunnies knew we were being tailed, but not Earl.

Not Arden either, apparently. When the cutoff came for the gully, she waved her arm around like General MacArthur and bumped down the road toward certain doom.

After the cutoff, though, the headlights kept on following the highway, and I started to relax a little. The dirt road wound around a small lake, then over to the gully and on past. When Earl and I pulled up to the edge of the cliff, Arden was already down on her knees, squinting along the beam of her flashlight, evaluating the facilities. They would do.

"Did you see those headlights, Arden?" I asked.

"What headlights?"

"The ones that tailed us for three miles."

"*Dear* Topaz," she said, squeezing my hand, then brushing past me to the bus. She sat in the front seat, looking through the tapes. I stuck my head in the door. "Tope, we are not breaking the law. We are innocent citizens on an outing. You are being paranoid."

"Just because you're paranoid doesn't mean they aren't out to get you."

"*Earl's* not being paranoid," she said, as if she were talking to one of the kids. Then she smiled.

"Earl wears a tie," I reminded her.

"You could wear a tie."

"I'd still be tall, black, and queer."

"Topaz," she stopped searching to look at me. "I wish you wouldn't call yourself that."

"I didn't invent it."

"No, but you perpetuate it." She started looking through the tapes again.

"They like Duke Ellington," I told her.

So she put Ellington on, and then she kissed me in a sisterly way, and said on our next adventure she would insist I wore a tie, and then she said she would wear one too.

We unloaded the cages and arranged them along the edge of the incline. Then we opened the doors and sat back cross-legged on the grass, letting them deliver themselves. It was because of the music that we didn't hear the car bearing toward us. Not until we were strafed by blinking blue lights did we hear, not until the young men in suits appeared, young men in ties, while the lightshow played and toyed over the disappearing ass of the last rabbit.

8

A CHARACTER REFERENCE

April 18, 1972

Dear Sirs:

You ask my opinion concerning the character of Miss Arden Benbow. Our paths have crossed several times. Our first encounter was over the matter of her name. As Assistant Registrar at the University it is my duty to review all requests—most of them I assure you quite routine—for name changes. Her petition dated January 3, 1971, requested that her name be changed on her records from Malthus to Benbow. Under "Reason" she had written, "Matrilinear succession."

I called her into my office, with every intention of accommodating her wishes, providing they fell within legal parameters. I assumed she was returning to her maiden name after her divorce, but when I asked her what her maiden name was, she said it was Ballinger, or some such.

"Then who, pray, is Benbow?"

"I am Benbow."

"By what authority?"

"Matrilinear succession."

It seemed her grandmother's maiden name was Benbow, that she was an Indian from somewhere in the northwest.

Well, my hands were tied, as I explained to Miss Benbow. Or Mrs. Malthus, as she then legally was. She has since—as I understand it—adopted her grandmother's name by action of the courts. Off the record, I find that kind of whimsy quite surprising in a woman who is the mother of eight or nine children. They can hardly know to whom they belong.

But as to my second encounter with the defendant, it concerned renewal of her fellowship for the next academic year. Miss Benbow—rather, Mrs. Malthus—was the present recipient of the Mabel Todd Huntington Fellowship for "young ladies who support American ideals." As Mrs. Huntington's nephew, I am a permanent ex officio member of the fellowship committee. Now usually I do not claim an active role in the Fellowship's administration, but this year I had no alternative.

I recommended to the committee that Mrs. Malthus's request for renewal be denied. Let me emphasize that this was not an easy decision, and I have been under no inconsiderable pressure from the Graduate English Program as a consequence.

First, let me make it perfectly clear that I did not oppose Mrs. Malthus's candidacy, as has been alleged, because she habitually parked her motorcycle in my staff parking space. True, I was forced to bring the matter to her attention, but once I made my feelings known, she kindly complied with my requests. There was some rumor of her having then shifted to the Dean of Graduate Studies' space, but I cannot testify concerning its veracity.

My objections have no such ephemeral base but are solely a response to the spirit of my late aunt's behest: that the Fellowship be awarded to "young ladies who support American ideals." Mrs. Malthus has violated this spirit on four occasions.

Mrs. Malthus is a self-avowed homosexual, a fact requiring no commentary by me. That she is the mother of seven throws a particularly grotesque light on the matter, if I may hazard a private opinion.

Mrs. Malthus has in her employ one of her kind, a male homosexual, whose job it is to assist in the raising of those unfortunate innocents. That Mr. Topaz happens to be black is of not the slightest import to me.

What does concern me, aside from his sexual preference, is that he tried this fall to bilk the Student Loan Office of $2000 by applying for aid under two names: Wilson Topaz and Topaz Wilson. His only defense was that as the University had taught him to answer to Topaz Wilson, it was the University's obligation to support Topaz Wilson. We did not prosecute.

The deciding piece of evidence came from an unexpected source. I was visited by a Sergeant Melvin Berkowitz of the Federal Narcotics Agency, who wanted information about Miss Benbow—that is, Mrs. Malthus—and Topaz Wilson . . . or rather Wilson Topaz. It seems they were arrested under suspicion of smuggling cocaine, but that the arresting officers—who dismembered Mrs. Malthus's vehicle with great thoroughness—could find no evidence of the drug.

It was Sergeant Berkowitz's belief that the cocaine was sequestered on rabbits which Mrs. Malthus, Mr. Topaz, and a friend released by night into the Malibu Hills. The sergeant had been thus far unable to capture any of the rabbits and so was at some pains to gather supporting evidence.

Though I subsequently learned these charges were dropped, it should be evident by now that Mrs. Malthus creates an atmosphere in which American ideals are not supported but assaulted.

Yours most sincerely,

Ellison Granville Todd

Ellison Granville Todd
Assistant Registrar

9

BREASTS, THIGHS, OR WINGS?

It is no exaggeration to say my uncle lay on the living room couch for nineteen years.

You are wondering what this detail of family life has to do with the issue of my fitness as a mother. If Uncle Groot had not risen from his couch after nineteen years, it is unlikely I would have taken that trip to Mexico with Aunt Vi.

I am talking about the trip of July 4, 1959, alluded to in several documents as an "abduction." Let me emphasize that there were no formal charges made. Ever. Only dark insinuations which thirteen years later I now answer by explaining how Aunt Vi and I became traveling companions.

Now you cannot possibly understand this trip without some attention to what went before. Things are connected, you know. Human events are all linked by a brilliant network of feelings, beliefs, ideas that wink on and off like Christmas tree lights. And time is the Christmas tree.

I think as children we always called my uncle by his last name because when we went to visit he was always inert. So we called him Uncle Groot as a mark of respect, and revered him as if he were a noted flagpole sitter. There he would lie, wearing an undershirt and postal service trousers, with his stocking feet propped up on one arm of the couch and his head nestled in the other.

Invariably he was unshaven. From a mysterious dark bottle housing a murky solution—20 percent alcohol and smelling like Lysol—he nipped from time to time. For his lung condition, Aunt Vi would explain for him, him, as if he had lost the power of speech years ago. Sometimes he might look up at us and grunt, but mostly he worked crossword puzzles from dog-eared paperbacks, listened to soap operas on the radio, or entered contests.

He entered every contest there was, and not just once if he could help it. From the grocery store Aunt Vi would wrestle home boxes of cereal, laundry detergent, cans of soup, dog food, cartons of Dr. Pepper the friendly pepper-upper. In their garage stood cases of unused goods with their box tops pried off or their entry forms gnawed out by Uncle Groot's penknife during the long afternoons of his confinement. Aunt Vi would send us home with mutilated boxes of cookies, unlabeled cat foot, and flat soda pop.

Uncle Groot had once worked, but it was before I was born. He was a mail sorter in Pacoima whose single ambition was early retirement. My mother told me he had approached the problem several ways: mysterious backaches, buzzing in his ears, flashes of light in his left eye. At last his lungs came through. A doctor friend diagnosed it as emphysema, and Uncle Groot took to the couch, subsidized by a small disability pension, thereby avoiding a lot of tedious labor, not to mention a world war.

This was of course in the days of radio, but inertia did not begin with television. No, television was only a welcome refinement. Uncle Groot made the transition from radio to television with ease, if not style. For Uncle Groot did have style, as we later discovered. But I am getting ahead of my story.

We will leave Uncle Groot lying on his couch, taking gentle pulls at his brown bottle, and watching Lord Blears meet Gorgeous George for the best two out of three, on a tiny greenly glowing screen.

Aunt Vi, for her part, spent these years in furious activity. She had worked for a living since she was sixteen: first as a Yo-Yo painter, then as an usherette in Grauman's Chinese Theater, then as a cake icer in a large commercial bakery in Atwater. It was said that she could ice a cake in three strokes.

Aunt Vi never seemed to consider her husband's behavior remarkable. His needs were minimal. She provided the cases of contest food, envelopes and stamps, and in return he interfered in her life not at all. In some ways it was an ideal marriage.

What threw everything out of balance was Uncle Groot's decision to get off his couch. It happened shortly before Christmas of '56. Uncle Groot was watching "Howdy Doody." Now Uncle Groot watched "Howdy Doody" every day of his life, but this time skyrockets were destined to go off in his astonished brain. He was lethargically watching a commercial of a four-year-old child baking cookies in a battery-powered oven, "just like Mommy's." I guess it was nearly three decades of contest entries that finally fanned the all but extinguished pilot light of ambition into a bonfire in my uncle.

That evening when Aunt Vi got back from the bakery, Uncle Groot was not on his couch. Later she told my mother that for a moment she thought he'd been stolen. She followed a trail of bulbs, belts, and electrical cords out to the garage where Uncle Groot was re-enacting the awful drama of the American Dream. He was inventing—he explained with a curious luminosity about the eyes—the vacuum cleaner.

Gently Aunt Vi broke the news to him that the vacuum cleaner had already been invented. And in fact there was for evidence her own, strewn there about the garage floor. Yes, he knew all that and could explain about her vacuum cleaner. It had become a model; it was a sacrifice to science; humanity was to benefit. He was inventing a miniature vacuum cleaner for little girls. It was to be called the Ti-Delight, emphasizing the innate relationship between tidiness and joy, where women are concerned. Toy manufacturers would beat a path to his door.

They did, strangely enough. Or more precisely, after the Ti-Delight vacuum cleaner was perfected, Uncle Groot climbed out of his postal department trousers and undershirt and into a charcoal gray Jim Clinton suit, a pink shirt with French cuffs, and finished up with a discreet pink and gray striped tie. Then he caught the Red Car downtown (that was when Los Angeles still had both a downtown and public transportation) with the Ti-Delight tucked lovingly under his arm. He returned with a contract, a generous one, one that would alter his and Aunt Vi's lives beyond imagining.

First they gave all the furniture to the Goodwill. Even the couch. New furniture arrived, Chinese Modern, I think they called it in the fifties. Then Uncle Groot had a wall knocked out, rooms added on, other fitful alterations made until there was only one solution possible: a new house. They moved to Sherman Oaks, acquiring a maid and a swimming pool.

Each morning Uncle Groot dressed himself with increasing care and even taste. In time he discarded his red socks and his boxer shorts decorated with files of moving red ants. He learned about wine. He mastered the cha-cha-cha. He took a mistress.

Now Aunt Vi went along with all this up to a point. But Uncle Groot could not prevail on her to quit being a cake girl, though by now she was nearly sixty. Uncle Groot, a little younger, was in his mid-fifties and therefore in his prime, according to popular belief. He preferred, quite naturally, to consider his spouse over the hill.

It is difficult, nevertheless, to account for his preoccupation with his wife's retirement. Unless he felt an inexplicable desire to know that *someone* was on that couch. He might have felt a touch guilty at leaving his post. Whatever the reason—perhaps a sense of embarrassment at having an aging cake girl for his wife—he was determined that she should set aside her icing knife forever.

Uncle Groot alone could never have prevailed. His cause was finally won with the complicity of nature. Aunt Vi had a mild stroke one afternoon between the devil's food cakes and the lemon tortes. She spent several days in a fashionable private hospital and was advised at discharge time by a solemn doctor faintly resembling Marcus Wellby that it was imperative she quit work and rest quietly at home.

Uncle Groot could not do enough for my Aunt Violet.

He had her bedroom redecorated, installed a Jacuzzi whirlpool bath, bought her the first color television ever, and the largest sectional couch I have ever seen. He wanted his sister, Margaret, to move in as a companion because his new position as executive vice president of Funtoys (as well as the increasing needs of his young mistress) demanded long absences from home.

Aunt Vi would not hear of it. There was, after all, the maid. She did, after all, have family of her own to look in from time to time.

Actually she had a plan. Inertia was not her style. Across the street lived my aunt's favorite neighbor, Maude Calisher. Maude was a very successful businesswoman. Very successful. She had a fleet of trucks driven by women who made the rounds to all the aircraft plants during coffee breaks and lunchtime, dispensing Twinkies, indifferent pastrami sandwiches, Fritos, Dr. Pepper, and other indigestibles. This trade, as Aunt Vi well knew, was not the sole source of Maude Calisher's enviable income. Maude Calisher was a bookie.

Each of her drivers carried a tiny notebook from which, at regular intervals, she read to her employer over a pay telephone. It was a simple but highly efficient system.

In jig time my aunt and Maude Calisher had worked out to their mutual satisfaction the details of the plan. Aunt Vi would receive the phone calls, recording the bets in code on tiny slips of paper. Maude, freed from record keeping, could attend now to the subtler details of her rapidly expanding enterprise. At five-thirty every afternoon she would collect the bits of paper from Vi, slip them into her Playtex Living Girdle, and have a poolside martini or two with her friend, before going home to dinner.

Not long after this pact was made, I dropped by to see how Aunt Vi was bearing her confinement. She came to the door herself, waving the maid away in annoyance, and folded me in her arms. She was wearing Turkish trousers of a midnight blue, over that a loose-fitting blouse with Indian patterns of rust and mauve, and a sash at the waist. Her white, unruly hair was tied up in a scarf and at her throat jangled heathenish-looking coins. She was every inch a gypsy. I was stunned with her. So large and outlandish was she, so radiant.

We sat down—Aunt Vi carefully avoiding the couch—and admired one another.

"And how are you?" she asked in that wonderfully resonant voice.

"Well, school. You know. There's not much to say about school. I'm so tired of it, Aunt Vi, so goddamned tired."

The phone rang, and I was glad. I could hear my voice begin to lapse into a schoolgirl whine. It was a tone I hated. I wanted my voice to be proud and resonant as Aunt Vi's. When she got back and settled herself I resolved to beat back the whine.

"You were saying about school . . . ?"

"Oh, just that I'm getting my B.A. this June, and that I'm ready, and that I wish people still went out to seek their fortunes, because I would."

"Oh, they still do," she corrected. "Absolutely, yes, every day, Arden." Then she looked thoughtful. "I'm still seeking mine."

The phone rang. She smiled. "I'll explain," she said simply.

In a few moments she returned. "I've gone into a new line of work."

"But I thought you weren't supposed to work anymore. Because of your heart." She looked through me, as if I hadn't spoken, or as if she were not listening to Uncle Groot in his imprecations, or as if she were ignoring a male chorus of doctors. She was teaching me then how to discount such voices. I knew it at the time—but felt awkward and corrected for having said it in the first place.

"I've become a bookie."

"A bookie!" I exploded.

"Exactly," she said with immense satisfaction. Rising, she motioned me into a small room off her bedroom that had always been her reading room, the place where she stored and enjoyed her romances and her *National Geographic*s. Newly added was an oversize French provincial desk against the far wall and a bright yellow telephone with four buttons, as well as miscellaneous pencils, erasers, paper clips, and bits of paper in some disarray.

Just then the phone rang. "Hello, Chicken Little." My aunt sat down absently, pulling a scrap of paper toward her. "Yes, now let me verify that. You want chicken for five, with cole slaw, mashed potatoes, but no gravy." At this point the other button lit up. "May I put you on hold?" she asks of the first caller. "Thank you. Chicken Little. Will you hold?" She returns adroitly to the first order. "Now did you want breasts, thighs, or wings? Fine. Thank you very much." Back to the second caller. I was watching my aunt seek her fortune.

I was afraid to ask her if there was any danger, because I began to glimpse the principle that safety and comfort were of limited appeal now, that she had somehow outstripped them, leaving them feeling faint at some roadside rest. But of course she read my thoughts: I was, after all, her favorite niece.

"There's nothing to worry about, dear. Everything is in code, you know." She laughed her wonderful low laugh. "Breasts, thighs, or wings means win, place, or show. It's all code. That's the beauty of it." She shook her coins in amusement and I laughed with her. "And then there's always Operation Failsafe." Her eyes narrowed and danced. "If the fuzz comes, I'm to flush the evidence down the johnny."

Now to properly understand this story you must pause here for a moment, letting the image of Aunt Vi seep from your conscious mind into your subconscious. She stood on an oriental rug from which the blues surrounding the rich and ancient burgundy sprang into her Turkish trousers. She shook the golden coins encircling her treasure map of a neck. "If the fuzz comes," she said with a toss of the head, "I'm to flush the evidence down the johnny."

The pity was that when the fuzz finally did come, my aunt forgot to flush the evidence down the johnny. She remembered to invite them in, she remembered to offer them warm sake (they had never tasted it before), but she did not, alas, remember those incriminating bits of evidence strewn so gaily about the French provincial desk.

Her night in Lincoln Heights Jail she accounts among the most memorable and pleasurable of her life. Not since leaving the bakery had she been nourished by such delicious stories. According to Aunt Vi, she sat up all night with a forger, a con artist, a hooker, and an arsonist, swapping stories.

Maude Calisher's memory of the night is not as pleasant as my aunt's, but then Maude Calisher got three to ten years in Sybil Brandt Correctional Institution for Women while Violet Groot was released into my uncle's custody and put on probation for three months.

I think, however, that she would have cheerfully exchanged places with Maude for the prospect of having the same kind of entertaining company she had enjoyed that memorable night in Lincoln Heights Jail. Uncle Groot's establishment in Sherman Oaks was doubtless more comfortable, but there were no stories and no employment.

I visited my aunt from time to time, sometimes with my mother, but I preferred going alone, and I think Aunt Vi preferred it too. My visits and the monthly trips to her probation officer—she forbade my uncle to accompany her—were oases in an otherwise desert existence.

Now, to the dynamic person inactivity is very taxing and can lead directly to heart failure, stroke, or cancer. Retiring industrialists seldom survive their first round of golf. It was the same with my aunt, who had been first a dynamic cake icer and after that a dynamic bookie.

I am sure the arresting officers felt they were protecting society from my aunt, when actually my aunt needed protecting from society. It was unhealthy for her not to hear the yellow phone calling gaily from the next room, it was unhealthy not to answer "Chicken Little," and it was unhealthy not to be visited every afternoon by Maude Calisher in her Playtex Living Girdle. It was society's fault that she had a massive stroke late one morning. Did the maid not find her slumped over her yellow phone?

When I got to the hospital she was sleeping, I guess. It was hard to tell. There were miles of clear tubing pumping fluids into her arms, and even a tube winding into her nostril, like some forlorn freeway exit to nowhere. Uncle Groot, who in his haste had brought along his mistress, was pacing around the room, accosting anyone in white, demanding explanations. An explanation as to why she slept so long (was she really breathing?), an explanation why there was no T.V. in the room, an explanation of what was in the suspended bottles, of where was the first nurse, the one here when she was admitted. He kept bumping into chairs and upseʹtting vases of flowers. His mistress, a young woman of about twenty-six or so, looked by turns horrified, then embarrassed, and finally bored. Uncle Groot did not notice. I went home.

Through phone calls to my mother I charted my aunt's slow progress: she could eat, with help; she could sit up a little; she had some bowel and bladder control. At first Uncle Groot planned to take care of Aunt Vi at home. With his customary relish for redecoration, he had the Jacuzzi torn out and replaced with a physical therapy pool, he bought a mechanical hospital bed with elaborate switches to control its contours, he bought an even larger T.V., he had kitchen and bathroom counters ripped out and lowered to wheelchair height, he had the toilet (the one into which Aunt Vi had not cast the evidence) encircled with safety bars. He bought a van with hydraulic lift, then hired three around-the-clock private nurses, selected—my mother alleged—for their looks.

My aunt made it her immediate business on returning home to fire the three nurses, each in her turn. By nightfall my aunt was unattended, a fact which drove Uncle Groot into a rage. He found her propped up in her mechanical bed with a clipboard wedged under a pillow for steadiness, while with her right hand she traced scrawls across lined notebook paper. She was learning to write. She would be, she told him, a novelist.

Next day Uncle Groot dispatched Aunt Vi to a nursing home in Thousand Oaks. I had rather ambivalent feelings about this shift in strategy, but there was the single advantage that I felt her more accessible to me. Wednesday seemed the most inconspicuous time for a visit, a day miles from any weekend, when the only people out and about in the early afternoon would be vagrants or housewives. Not to mention recent college graduates, whose dubious ranks I had joined some weeks before.

Also, by this time I had met Malthus at the Griffith Park Planetarium, duly noted his resemblance to William Holden, and heard his lecture on the rotation of the earth on its axis. We had seen several art films at the Sunset Theater, innumerable free travelogues at the Wilshire Ibel, and had dined once at Nick's Grotto, twice at the Doggie Emporium. I felt my attraction to him was insane. Ours was a relationship that kept coming back marked "Insufficient Funds," yet I persisted in drawing on the account.

I decided to go to Mexico for the summer, or for a while, anyway. But Malthus gave me a forty-minute lecture on bacteria of the region and I lost all desire to travel. I decided to buy a Harley Davidson and he showed me statistics on cranial injuries in cycle accidents. There was a kind of vacuity about myself, about L.A., and about the summer itself. What was there to do, except seek out the less reputable members of one's family?

So it was a hot Wednesday afternoon, and the rusty white Dodge Dart I had borrowed from my roommate had been threatening vapor lock since the Thousand Oaks exit. I pulled into the parking lot of the rest home, turned off the engine, and shuddered with it several times. Heat was rising from the asphalt in shimmers of steam. Off in a corner I could see the blue van Uncle Groot had bought. Afraid I might run into him, despite my planning, I walked over to check it out. The van had obviously been there unused for several days. Windows were up, doors locked, no personal effects, and a delicate layer of powdered smog lightly covered the bright new paint. It was just a piece of inert apparatus.

I was walking around to the side window, for a last look, when I felt the asphalt ripple under my feet. Or thought I did. It might have been the heat, producing a human analogue of vapor lock. But I didn't think so. It felt like something outside myself, exerting itself. A tremor. Zigging and zagging through my body.

When it ended I felt a kind of energized exhaustion, the way you feel after a long swim. That kind of cleanness. I put out my hand to steady myself, touching the van momentarily, then withdrawing from the scorch. The heat and hardness of the surface reminded me, called me back.

I started toward the entrance, vaguely aware of the freeway hum, aware then it had never ceased. Had the charge gone through anyone but me? Not being a poet yet, I felt reluctant to call it an earthquake if no one else had felt it.

Inside I asked the receptionist if she had noticed anything unusual, and she looked at me—poised in the middle of filing her nails—as if I might be a patient, misplaced.

"An earthquake, for example?" I smiled.

"Afraid not, honey." She went back to her filing.

"Well, could you tell me where Violet Groot is?"

She looked at me as if everything was now explained. "Mrs. Groot is in the Eisenhower wing, room 12."

"Mrs. Groot is a Democrat," I advised her.

"Mrs. Groot is a patient."

I hated to let her have the last word. I put her on my list and headed in the direction indicated by the tapered nail.

10

MEMOIRS OF THE GREAT CARBONARA

June 21, 1959

Here begin the memoirs of Maurio Carbonara.

Mrs. Groot gets the credit for that line. I never could of thought of it myself. See, yesterday was my birthday and she gives me this notebook.

"Look, Homer," she says, "write what I tell you on the first page."

She is lying in her bed kind of jacked up, with her head fallen over to one side. I fix her pillow so she can get her eyes on me. At least one of them, anyhow.

"Write this," she says, once I get her sitting right. She closes her eyes, only has to think a second, and out it comes, top of her head. "Here begin the memoirs of Maurio Carbonara."

"Who in hell is Maurio Carbonara?" I ask her. "I mean, it's a swell name and all, Mrs. Groot . . . "

"Violet," she corrects me.

"Violet, I mean. But I'm Homer. You know that. Homer Rice." See, I'm an orderly in this rest home and I'm all the time meeting people who think they're Jesus H. Christ or Joan of Ark or something. And that's mostly fine with me. They're entitled. And besides, it for sure don't come out a my paycheck. But Mrs. Groot always looked like she knew what end was up. So I was kind a surprised at her forgetting who I was and all, because we been friends like for a couple a weeks.

I sneak her a beer now and then, and help her with her writing. See, she had a stroke and is kind a bummed up. First time she asked me for a beer I didn't know should I give it or what. Had one a those plastic contraptions hooked onto her for collection, as it was. Finally I say what the hell, so those bums on the next shift got to empty it a couple a times. But she's been coming along real fast. Says it's the beer. She can sit up in her chair and talk pretty good through the side of her mouth. Wants me to get her some Kinney sticks out a P.T. to practice walking at night, but Nurses' Station will have my ass if they find out. You better believe it.

Anyway, I was saying about this Carbonara business, "But I'm Homer Rice." It's after lunch and the trays from my wing are back downstairs, so I got not much else to do for twenty minutes or so, and Mrs. Groot's always got a story or two in her.

"Well, Maurio," she says, pulling herself up on the exercise bar hanging over her bed.

"Homer," I say real soft.

"Maurio," she goes on like she don't hear good, but I know she does, "you tell me you are a magician."

"Actually, Mrs. Groot, I used to work as a magician's assistant."

"It's the same thing, Maurio."

"Not to Mr. Vincenti."

"Mr. Vincenti?"

"My boss. The Amazing Vincenti. He said I was too little and my hands was too big and my grammar was *unmentionable*. He said I was the punishment God sent him for drinking. He said I'd never make a thing of myself without I grew six inches and learned to keep my mouth shut."

"But you are a powerful person, Maurio."

She says this like it's a fact everybody knows. And she's got this voice like honey. Sixty if she's a day.

"I used to work out," I tell her.

Then she makes this gesture like I can go now, like I ain't been doing as good as I ought to in my lessons, and she starts chinning herself on her exercise bar. So I go off to empty Mr. Rattling's bag.

June 22, 1959

Violet says I should write in this book every day, otherwise I will lose it.

"Lose what?" I ask.

"Your inspiration." She smiles at me. I brought her the Kinney sticks today, wrapped up in sheets on a cripple cart. And a Coors. She says she will practice only when I am off duty, not to get me in trouble. I tell her me and trouble are drinking buddies.

"Do you know what inspiration is, Maurio?" she says, popping the cap, and gesturing with the can. "Inspiration is the power used to make one thing out of another." She waits, taking a long pull off the can, looking satisfied. "Consider this beer, for instance."

What now? I think. Sometimes she starts these things when I ain't got the time. Right now I'm supposed to be mopping the bathroom floors. It's my head, you know, shit job that it is. But still I'm wanting to hear. I don't know why.

"Now beer," she says, "is made out a malt, wheat, hops . . . and who knows what?" (Sometimes she starts out strong in facts, and then she runs dead out, but she ain't the one to let that get her down.) "Then they ferment it, and mull it around, and ferment it some more, and then when the time is right, voila! Beer!"

This thought seemed to make her happy.

"I got to mop the johns," I say.

June 23, 1959

Well, today was my day off. What do I do but go to MacArthur Park with my old lettuce and feed the ducks? Homer Rice, I say to myself, is this the best you got to do with yourself on your day off? I look over at this dish on the next blanket. She's reading a book. What can I tell her? That I used to be a magician's assistant? That before that I sold bait in my mother's bait store? That I am five foot four in my stocking feet? That I am losing my hair? What am I supposed to write in this book?

June 24, 1959

I asked Violet what I am supposed to be writing.
She says, "Well, what have you been writing?"
"Oh, just what I do."
"Fine. Now write what you think about what you do. Ferment it. Like the beer." She laughs at the idea. "You can put anything you like in there, Maurio, really. The book and the name are a gift from me."

June 25, 1959

First thing I hear at morning report is Violet makes it down to the sun-room on her own steam about 2 A.M. and falls into the T.V., which crashes around her like demolition derby. Whole Eisenhower wing in an uproar. The night nurse finds the Kinney sticks. Vi covers for me, says she lifted them from the dining room. I think they got my number but won't say so on account a not wanting old man Groot to kick up a fuss. So everybody's glad to dummy up. This time.

June 27, 1959

Next time I see Violet she's got one a those mechanical wheelchairs and is zipping down the hall toward the sun-room. I hand her the *Times* with a can of Coors wrapped up inside. She asks me have I got a minute. We settle behind the philodendron.

"Dear Maurio," she says, "I hope I did not get you in any trouble. I tripped over a fucking bedpan."

"No," I tell her, "that's OK, Violet. No sweat." And I mean it. For a minute there, all the time piled into that one quiet place. We just smiled and smiled.

Then she says to me, "Maurio, I need a few things." I get scared, kind of. Then I beat it off.

"Wheat germ," she says.

"Wheat germ?"

"Yes, and desiccated calves' liver, dolomite, calcium, C and E, maybe a touch of zinc. That ought to do it."

"You building something?"

"You might say so, Maurio. Yes, that describes it very well."

June 29, 1959

Yesterday was my day off and I go where Violet sends me, to this health food store on Ventura Boulevard. There is this girl in baggy white pants with a purple band tied around her forehead and a baggy white blouse you could see through without trying. I guess she is maybe twenty-five and not much taller than me, a nice thing when it happens, which ain't often. I am feeling kind a weird in there because I don't know what I am doing, and anyhow I tend to be shy on account a growing up over a bait shop and all.

So I am standing in front a something called Tiger Milk, holding the
list Violet wrote out for me. "I'm Gloria," the girl in baggy pants says,
"can I be of any assistance?" I hand her the list. We go around getting
the stuff, and she suggests some more. (I run up quite a bill, but Violet
is good for it.) The girl asks me am I an athlete and I tell her no, it's for
a friend.

"You look like an athlete," she says.

"I used to work out," I tell her. Which is the truth. In high school I
was too little for football or basketball, so I went out for gymnastics.
Placed fourth in rings, statewide.

Then, not knowing I am going to, I say, "Actually, I'm a magician."

July 1, 1959

Violet has a lot of visitors. Most the people around here got one foot
in the grave. Nobody wants to see them. Unless they got money or some-
thing. Course, a lot of them do. Violet's got money but she's OK.

Her husband comes once a week. Twice, tops. My idea of an asshole,
you ask me. Tells everybody what to do, and wants it done now. Some-
times comes in with that tart of a secretary. I try not to be around. If it's
Sunday, he's got to turn on the baseball. Violet hates baseball. I try not
to be around.

The others I mostly like. Her sister's swell. Best I like the girls from
the bakery. "Here's the cake girls!" says Violet, and settles back for stories.
She loves a story.

Well, yesterday the cake girls had came and went. Violet's supposed to
be resting but instead she has me helping her with her wheelchair engine,
souping it up, you know. Violet likes action.

Anyway, we got the parts spread out all over the foot of the bed, with
a sheet handy so we can cover up the whole shebang if anybody comes
in on us. Violet's in her chair drinking a Coors. I'm about to step up the
idle when there is this shaking, and I look at her to see does she feel it
too. "Quake," she says, looking pleased. Then it stops.

Across the corridor I can hear Mrs. Wall listening to "As the World
Turns." Nobody yells. Nothing. It's like it didn't happen. Except to Violet
and me. She shrugs.

Just then the door bangs open and I make a jump for the tools. But
I see it is OK. Pretty soon there is lots of hugging and kissing and Violet
is introducing me.

"Arden, this is my very dear friend, Maurio Carbonara. Maurio, my niece, Arden Benbow. Maurio is a magician."

"Well, I ain't worked at it for years," I say looking down. Then I see my big hands and put them around back, out a sight. But this Arden's got her right hand out for a shake, and so there ain't nothing to do but oblige. She's kind of on the tall side but pretty—you know?—and she's got this voice like Violet's. But not quite. Violet sounds like the old moon and Arden sounds like a new one. Just a sliver of a moon, but a moon anyhow.

"Arden is a poet," Violet tells me. Now Arden blushes and looks out the window.

I say I got to go now (not wanting to butt in on family and all), but Violet tells me no, this concerns me too. For the life a me I don't see what she's got in mind, but I finish up the chair quick and put away the tools and then sit down on the edge of the bed to see what's got Violet on her hind legs.

"Arden," she says in that silvery voice, "what are your plans for the summer?" One side a her face is still somewhat froze up. Nothing to speak of. She is still one hell of a good-looking woman.

It's pretty clear from the way Arden shifts around in her chair that she had not give the thing too much thought or that she can't make up her mind. Who can? Nobody these days can say what they want until they've gone and done something different anyways. The same with Arden. But she is going to tell her aunt the first thing that pops into her head.

"Well, I was thinking of going to Mexico."

"Excellent!" says Violet, so quick and whole-hearted that her niece kind a stops breathing for a minute. "Maurio and I would like to come along."

Now it's my turn for a surprise. But I play it cool. I figure she is revved up about the earthquake, maybe, or because her niece is visiting. So I'll just wait it out. But she honestly don't look revved, now I take a closer look. Arden looks revved, but Violet looks easy as you please. She's twinkling but she's easy as an old catfish in deep water.

By now Arden is starting to get her words together, and out come a string of "I just don't see how we can possibly's" and so forth.

"Nonsense, nonsense," says Violet, waving away Arden's words like so many cobwebs in her path. She reaches in the pocket of her leopard-skin bathrobe and feels around some (her right hand still don't work all that good), and then she is holding aloft in front of me and Arden a flashing set a car keys.

11

INGENUE

Actually I'm grateful to have the chance to explain this to anybody at all. I never even had a regular hearing. They just suspended me. Then they fired me.

Then I couldn't pay for my acting lessons, I fell behind in my rent, I couldn't get my hair done and the roots started to show. It was that bitch's fault.

I marked her for a troublemaker right away. The first time I ever laid eyes on her she made a smart ass (excuse me) remark. The aunt was a troublemaker too.

Oh, I should explain who I am. I'm Wanda Holbrook from Rock Island (formerly). I wait tables at Laurie's House of Prime Ribs (on the Strip). But then—this was, what? twelve, thirteen years ago—I was studying acting mornings, and afternoons (from three to ten) I was a receptionist at Thousand Oaks Rest Home (privately owned). On account of this incident my whole career in movies vanished before my eyes. All on account of that crazy old lady and her niece (crazy, too, if you ask me).

Her very first day at Thousand Oaks the old lady makes a scene. They assigned her to the Eisenhower wing. She's a Democrat, she says. Got to be having her way even if she can hardly talk. I explain nobody gets to choose where they're assigned. They're just assigned, and that's that. "More's the pity," she mumbles, being the type that's come-what-may got to have the last word.

Well, the next thing I hear about Mrs. Violet Groot is that her majesty has got drunk in the night and beat a T.V. set to pieces with her cane. I ask you.

Now maybe when I tell you I do not know how Violet Groot got out of there without anybody seeing, you just might believe me. Nobody else ever did. I know some of them thought I took a bribe, and some of them thought I was at least loafing in the coffee room when the three of them went out the front door that night.

If you ask me, I don't think they went out the front door at all. How did they get out? Ask that two-bit detective, Michael Raven. That's who.

12

THE JOURNAL OF MICHAEL RAVEN

July 4, 1959

I arrived at the Thousand Oaks Rest Home as per Mr. Groot's request at 10:30 P.M. The police had just terminated their preliminary investigation. They are satisfied, after interrogating staff and several patients, that Mrs. Groot left of her own volition at about 9:00 P.M., assisted by an orderly named Homer Rice and Mrs. Groot's niece, Arden Benbow. There is some question regarding Mrs. Groot's sanity.

Sargeant Lazlo Trumpkin investigated the lawn outside the French door leading from Mrs. Groot's room. He found no foot impressions, except those of the Japanese gardener. Examination of the other patients' doors yielded similar results. The remaining exits are: three fire exits equipped with automatic alarm devices, and the main entrance, staffed at the time of Mrs. Groot's departure by a young woman named Wanda Holbrook.

July 5, 1959

Three Interviews

#1 Wanda Holbrook

Miss Holbrook may be concealing something. Obvious antagonism with both Mrs. Groot and her niece. Hinted at possibility of a political intrigue.

Provided the following descriptions:

Violet Groot
About 5'6", 62 years, white disheveled hair, partial paralysis of the right side, a cast in her right eye.

Arden Benbow
5'9" or so, 110 pounds, long dark hair, brown eyes. About 20 to 24 years. Hook nose.

Homer Rice
5'4", blue eyes, dirty blond receding hair, pronounced chest and arm muscles, narrow hips, huge hands. 38 years. Bad grammar. Looks like an ape.

#2 John Rattling

Mr. Rattling is a patient in the rest home. He observed Mr. Rice frequented Mrs. Groot's room, to the neglect of his duties. There he believes they drank whiskey, played cards, and examined pornographic materials. Occasionally in the night he was awakened by ecstatic cries. His complaints were unheeded, he avows, because of Mr. Groot's influence with the administration. He believes there is a gangland connection, possibly the Mafia. Rice sometimes went by the name of Maurio, probably his real name, said Rattling.

#3 Ida Wall

Mrs. Wall, another elderly patient, has the room directly across from Mrs. Groot's. She is particularly fond of Rice, "that nice young man." At meal times he did magic tricks for her. She believes Rice was a professional magician with the stage name The Great Fettucine. When asked if she had any ideas of the whereabouts of the three, she first hinted that Rice had made them all disappear. Then she recalled a *National Geographic* Mrs. Groot had showed her, describing the embalming techniques in Guanajuato, a village in Mexico. Mrs. Groot said she wanted to go there for some inspiration with her novel, a gothic romance, according to Mrs. Wall. Mrs. Groot had said, "You know, a good novel is 90 percent atmosphere," and Mrs. Wall had responded, "A good novel is 90 percent sex."

July 5, 1959
Hermosillo
Midnight

Mrs. G. and her confederates crossed the border at Nogales some time around 4 A.M. in a 1959 blue Ford van, well stocked with water, canned goods, and other equipment and provisions, as if for prolonged camping. The border guard said the van was driven by a young woman wearing a World War I aviator's helmet, that next to her sat a very short man of forty or forty-five, dressed in a black cape, and that lying in the back was an old woman ("la vieja") who winked at him when he shone the light in her face.

I am proceeding south on 15, confident of overtaking three such distinctive people, especially since they must travel slowly with the invalid lady.

13

RUBY'S CAMPGROUND AND TRAILER PARK

Michael Raven? Oh hell yes. But Jesus, that was a long time ago. Michael Raven.

Came dragging his tail in here one afternoon at siesta time. Car broke down. Ramón showed him in. Only Americans wander around during siesta time. No sense. Got to be doing, every blessed minute. So I knew he was American before he opened his mouth, not that he could say much when he did.

Ramón went off to get him a beer. Meanwhile I was giving Raven the once-over. Damn fine-looking man. Course there was a kind of gray look to him. Had Montezuma's revenge for days, it turned out. Even that couldn't keep him on his back where he belonged. Crazy Americans.

Course, I'm an American, too. Used to be known as Ruby Red from Frisco. Girl on the Red Swing? You might of heard about me. I'd swing right out over the street. Pack in those sailors, you can believe. That was during the war. First one.

You wouldn't think it to look at me, but I'm seventy. Yes, and still kicking. But anyway, when this Michael Raven strolls into my sitting room, I'm still in my fifties, retired from show business, owner and operator of Ruby's Campground and Trailer Park, Highway 15, just this side of Guaymas, State of Sonora.

Ramón gives him a Carta Blanca. Michael is wearing one of those summer suits that can't wrinkle. But Michael himself is so beat up from the

heat and the runs that the suit looks funny, like it's got no business look-
ing crisp. His shirt is likewise drip-dry but filthy, formerly Eisenhower
pink, and his tie is all pulled out of shape. I can see he is not used to
looking like he looks, and maybe not used to asking for help.

He reaches into an inside pocket and flips an I.D. in my general
direction.

"Hold on, hold on a minute," I say, reaching for the card before he
can bury it back inside his jacket. You got to keep your eyes open in
this life, a little something I picked up in Frisco. So I study the I.D. and
see he is a private dick working out of L.A. for some hotshot agency or
other. "Oh, a cop," I say. Just testing, you understand. He corrects me,
properly pissed, and I figure he is OK.

During my years in show business I can't say my doings with the fuzz
were of the best. One of the hazards of the job, you might say.

Now with private dicks you are in another ballpark because whoever
hires them usually is as anxious as you to stay clear of the law.

And besides, this guy is cute. I don't just mean looks, either.

Anyway, the beer is starting to cool him off and he is anxious to get
down to business, being that eager kind of person that still has got a lot
to learn. I can see he is going to get beat over the head some, things being
what they are. But I feel grateful to get to see him before the shine gets
taken off.

He asks me if there are any Americans at the campgrounds. I tell him
if there aren't, I'm in trouble. He says he means any checked in since the
fourth of July. Well, I am beginning to figure out he means Vi, Arden,
and Maurio. So while he's asking questions wide of the mark, I'm trying
to figure out how to shape my lie.

Actually I have an almost uncontrollable impulse to tell the truth.

That kind of upbringing is no asset, believe me. I was twenty before I
lied at all. Then I had to practice at it because pretty quick I found out
you couldn't survive otherwise. Now I think of it as a kind of art, like
first-rate costuming. So I'm good at it, but only if I can sketch it out in
my mind, and even baste it together a little. But to this day, pop a ques-
tion at me and I'm just as likely to tell the truth as anything.

I'm worried now that will happen. Because of my instincts, and be-
cause Michael is cute.

Now let me explain to you why I decided to lie to Michael.

You see, strippers are like athletes. They got to plan for early retirement. What I did after stripping and before retirement is nobody's business but my own. Let's just say I moved in high circles. Anyway, while I was a working woman I was a saving woman. Government bonds, mostly. But I wasn't getting anywhere that way, so I invested it. Never mind in what.

So when I turned fifty I jumped in the Grand Prix and headed south. It was this dream, you see, handsome and familiar as Cary Grant in a tuxedo. It had to do with Mexico and palm trees and luscious nights under the stars.

Don't laugh. If you had any sense, you'd celebrate every time somebody puts good money down on a dream.

Whenever the highway opened onto the coast, I'd pull on the brakes and run down to the Gulf, and wade around asking, "Is this it? Is this it?" I was almost to Guaymas when I found this place. The bungalow was falling to pieces and the garden was wild. It was perfect. That night I slept in the bungalow, right over there, on the floor. When I woke up, I could hear the tide coming in, and the breeze in the palm trees, and a little dog yapping down the beach, and I knew this was Ruby's Campground and Trailer Park.

From the garden I got bananas and mangoes that I took down to those rocks, right where the gazebo is now, and I sat down to eat, with my feet dangling in the water. Along came the yapping dog, and then his master, with a fishing pole. Turned out to be Ramón. Well, Ramón asks if I live here. And I say yes. Because the dream is so out of hand by now that I believe I do live here. One thing leads to another and he asks if I have a job for him. "What can you do?" I ask him. "Anything," he answers right back. I figure either he really can do anything or he is one hell of an accomplished liar, so I hire him. In time I find out both things are true.

All this happened maybe five years before Vi and her friends. Time they arrive the house is sound and clean and comfortable, the campgrounds are laid out, picnic tables built, electrical hook-ups and sewage provided for the trailers, showers installed, and the gazebo built down on the rocks, as I have said. The whole dream is running like clockwork. I am a little bored.

Now I don't want you to think I despise peace. After all, the point of the dream was probably peace. If you can say dreams have a point. Mostly I like peace. But I tend to appreciate it more if every now and then there's a little chaos folded in.

It's like this. Remember I was telling you about waking up at the bungalow that morning, and about listening to the water on the shore and all? Well, that was more peaceful to me the minute Ramón's dog started yapping down the beach. Something about extremes I do find so pleasing.

That's partly why the campground. Oh, there's the practical reason, though probably I could get by without the money. No, the real reason is I have people if I want them, and privacy if I want that. Sometimes I keep to myself a week at a time. Even Ramón stays away. Other times I'm down the road every night playing canasta in one trailer or another, or having folks up to the bungalow for a swell meal.

The thing about Vi was she got here when I was hard up for a little chaos. Four sites were empty, one was taken by a bunch of Youths for Christ on motorcycles. (The youths, I mean.) And the rest of the inmates were strictly geriatric. No offense.

Not that Vi was any spring chicken. Jesus, she was sixty if she was a day. Hobbled around on canes. You might of thought she couldn't have been much company. But she was.

They came at dusk, looking like a traveling circus. I was standing in the kitchen, facing out toward the road, with the Gulf just beyond, talking to Maria, Ramón's daughter.

Well, this van pulls up. Girl about twenty hops out wearing jeans, a Stetson with a beaded band, a T-shirt, her hair in a long Indian braid down her back. Then this midget jumps out the back, dressed in a black magician's cape over who-knows-what. Together they help an old lady out, and she is wearing some kind of flowing Oriental pants, a see-through blouse, with gold coins clinking all over her. They want a site right on the beach, they don't know for how long, and could they have some ice?

I show them to my best site, down close to the water, with a small stand of trees that makes a nice shelter. Ramón brings along a bucket of ice, and next thing you know the midget is pouring margaritas out of a shaker. We have some good talk, then I leave them to their supper, though it is hard to go, feeling as I do the fireworks are about to begin.

Back at the bungalow I read a while to wear off a little of the excitement. But the generator quits just as I am about to find out who the Count's real father is. Ramón yells in do I want him to fix it now, and I tell him morning's soon enough. So I light a candle and get in bed.

Clean sheets. Full moon. I can hear the tide raking through the shells on its way out, and I can hear through the palms the Youths for Christ playing guitars and singing hymns.

Next morning my eyes snap open around five o'clock. The older you get, the earlier you wake up. Some people hate it, but I cherish it. You have a chance to see how things look before everything starts to move. If you follow me.

So I have my coffee and a mango, then start out down the gravel road that winds through the campsites. A kerosene lamp or two on in the geriatric trailers. I glance over at the Youths for Christ and get a surprise. Usually of an evening they sing till about eleven, then they get into their Christian blanket rolls, sleep till eight, eat their cornflakes, tear their bikes apart all morning, and put them together all afternoon. Today they are not in their Christian blanket rolls. Every bike is gone, unless that pile of parts out beyond the tent is a bike. I know they have finally gone looking for a little chaos. It's like the coming of the blue van and its band of gypsies caused the wind to shift.

I start off to see them—my gypsies—hurrying like I have an appointment. Nobody is stirring that I can see, but when I get close suddenly somebody sits up, right on the roof of the van. It is the girl, Arden, and she looks like she is ready to jump the intruder. Then she recognizes me and laughs, falling back into her blankets, foam rubber, and pillows. Like into a nest. "Coffee?" I ask her, making no sound but just shaping out the word. She nods and starts to climb down the aluminum ladder, wearing only her skivvies.

The rear of the van is open like a whale's mouth. I can't help but look in. The old lady is sitting up in her sleeping bag, tossing coins into her lap, and making notes in the margin of a road map. "The I Ching," she explains to me.

Arden wrestles out her jeans and T-shirt, asks the old lady does she want coffee.

"You go along, dear. I'll take care of Maurio," she says, flicking her gypsy eyes in the direction of the sleeping midget.

So we are off to the bungalow, and it is still early morning, and I know it is happening.

We stop in the garden for mangoes. Arden holds out large hands. Then from the highway comes this God-awful sound. It is the Youths for Christ trying to outrun the Guaymas police. They squeal their bikes off the highway onto the dirt road, then down the path to their camp-sites, where there is revving of engines and considerable yelling, and in three minutes they lash clothes and sleeping bags onto their motorcycles. Then off again full tilt up 15 like mounted black dots against the morning sun. I never saw them set off to greater advantage.

Well, Arden and I missed that cup of coffee, but it was the only one we did miss. The days and nights had tides of peace and chaos, without me having to tinker with a thing. Mornings Arden and Ramón would work on the generator or the plumbing or whatnot. Vi and the midget did their body building. Lifted weights—would you believe it?—handmade weights Ramón and Arden put together out of old flywheels, bailing wire, and pipe joints. I can see them now, standing there on the beach, old lady and the dwarf hoisting up those weights like offerings to some old Mexican god or other.

About two we'd have lunch down at the gazebo. Maria would make one of her Indian dishes, and we'd all bring along fruit or cheese or wine. Whatever we had. Afterwards, Maurio would entertain us with a few magic tricks. Then we'd talk and get sleepy, going off one by one to siesta.

Afternoons were quiet, usually. Sometimes Vi and I would talk gothic romance. She was the only person I ever met who read more novels than I did, and remembered them all too. "Oh, yes," she'd say, "that was Allison Pemberton's *Secret of Waymouth Dungeon*." And we'd sit, recol-lecting until it felt like we lived inside the pages of all those novels, but making the trashy excitement into a better kind. Like all those lockets and crypts and charms and dark lurking men stood for something bigger than what they were.

Well, anyhow, I have gone on long enough about those sweet times to let you know why I was determined to lie to Michael Raven about my three friends. So while Michael circled in on the question, I got ready to spring my lie.

Timing is everything, moments like these. I must not be too quick, or too slow, or tell too much. I am kind of holding my breath and counting, like when I was the Girl on the Red Swing and would launch out over the street with all these sailors looking up. But just as I am ready for flight, the door perfectly bursts open and there stands Arden Benbow, jiggling with excitement, smudges from head to toe, finished off with a smear of grease under her lip that looks like nothing so much as half a handlebar moustache.

"Oh, Jesus, Ruby," she says, "I'm sorry. I didn't know you had company." Then she turns to Michael, who is sitting on the couch looking kind of gray green again, and walks over, holding out a greasy hand to him in welcome. "Arden Benbow," she says, with the smile of a baby.

Michael looks catatonic. Poor son of a bitch wanted to spend days watching with binoculars from behind trees. Throw a little style into it, you know? Whole thing has become ridiculous. So he holds out his hand, and gives hers a sorry kind of a shake. "Michael Raven," he says, like he can't quite believe this information himself. Then he examines his greasy hand and stuffs it into his pants pocket.

Now Ramón comes in and he is almost as ragtag as Arden. They have been building a motorcycle out of that heap of junk left by the Youths for Christ. It runs. They are excited. They hop around the room. Ramón is waving a bottle of tequila under Michael's nose, telling him it will cure the runs.

Into this circus stumps Vi on her two canes, gold coins jingling about her wrists. "The Queen of Swords!" she yells, like she is answering a question on a quiz show. She has been into the Tarot again.

"This is Michael," I tell her. "Michael is a private detective," I say, lowering my eyelids real slow, so she will not miss the point.

"How fascinating," she says, sitting down next to him, and commences telling him about her night in Lincoln Heights Jail.

"Michael is employed by your husband," I interrupt, not bothering with the eyelids this time.

Vi stops here and stares at Michael. Ramón sets the tequila bottle down. Arden crosses over and stands at her aunt's right hand, as if she finally recognizes the intruder she has watched for every blessed night from the top of the van.

There is a long silence. A few barks drift up the beach. Then nothing.

Finally Vi says, pulling herself very straight, under the circumstances, "Well, young man, and what have you got to say for yourself?"

"Ma'am?" says Michael, looking confused. Vi repeats her question. Michael ahems and tries coaxing the knot of his dirty tie back into place. Then he starts out quietly explaining the purpose of private detectives, the credentials of his company, his training, his dedication. Pure horse shit.

Violet knows it. She waves her hand like she is clearing the air. Then she reaches down for her canes. Michael leans to help, but Violet is too quick. She hoists herself up, and I can see the body building is beginning to pay off. She has kind of a V-shape, small but strong, like a Japanese acrobat. Partly it is that she is pissed, but mostly it's the body building.

At this point Michael gets to his feet, out of a kind of automatic politeness, but he is unsteady from days and nights of the runs. He lurches. It is pretty clear he is going over like a tree in a forest. Vi is nearest but she can't catch him on account of her canes. So Arden closes in, and for a second it looks like he is falling too fast, but she bags him neatly just before his head hits the coffee table. We lay him out on the couch. He could have passed for eight years old at that moment. Vi gives him a good long look, shakes her head, and stumps on out the door.

But she is not done with him. Not by a long way. Ramón and Arden drag him into the storage room at the back of the bungalow. There's a cot there and a world of trunks from my entertainment days and things Michael isn't in any position to mind. We make him comfortable as we can, clean him up, and keep trying to get liquids down him. Next morning Vi turns up, wanting to see Michael, says she has been thinking. I tell her Michael is still asleep and she says all the better. She sits in there on a stool for close to an hour, watching.

It turns out she has slipped the Tarot pack under his pillow, and the minute he wakes up he has got to listen to a reading. She is not being unkind; she has simply forgot about natural functions like eating and going to the bathroom, both at the moment much more important to Michael than to most people. So she tries to wait patiently, and finally we have them settled with a packing case between them. Violet has Michael cut the cards several times. Then she carefully lays them out in a cross pattern on the crates, and finishes up with a line of cards either side of the cross. I'm no expert but anyone can see the Death card is lying right on top the cross. Michael sucks in his breath.

"Ah, Death!" says Violet, fairly clapping her hands. Then she catches me giving her a hard look and notices that Michael has that dangerous greenish tinge to his face again. "Oh, no, no, no. Dear friends," she says, shaking her head slowly, like we are silly children. "Death is not a spiritual death," she says, as if that will make Michael feel fine again.

It doesn't. She tries again. "The Death card does not mean your disease is going to be fatal." Here she winks at Michael. "No, it means revitalization of the Life Force, it means change, transformation." She leans close to Michael, who is looking at me as if he is hoping I will get him out of this. "It means, Michael, you are going to slough off your old life and recreate yourself." She says this like he has just won a Buick Riviera on "Let's Make a Deal." Then she gives him an affectionate pinch on the arm, tells him good morning, and stumps on out the door, leaving the impression he has not seen the last of her.

Well, Michael spends three or four days in bed, then he is up and around but taking it easy. One day Ramón and Arden tow his car in from the highway. Michael has told them not to, but they do anyway, and after a couple of mornings they have it running pretty good, though of course the radio and three hub caps have long since disappeared into downtown Guaymas.

By now I am in the habit of just letting Vi carry on however she pleases. Still, I begin to wonder about this neighborly fixing of Michael's car and why they don't take this opportunity of giving Michael the slip. So finally I ask Vi straight out, which is my way, unless I have some obligation to lie, as I have explained before.

She has just finished her morning push-ups and we are both sitting on the tailgate of the van, dangling our legs. When I ask the question, she looks pleased, like it's the very question she was hoping I would ask. But she answers it with another question, something she often does, I have noticed.

"But dear, whyever should I want to lose Michael?"

"Because he's after you," I say, feeling like the straight man.

"The question is, What is he after me for? I doubt Michael knows that as well as I do." She looks mysterious for a minute. Then, looking more practical, she adds, "Besides, he's got nothing on me. What can he do? I wasn't committed to that nasty institution, I enrolled. Then I withdrew. That was my prerogative. Now I choose to travel in Mexico with my friends. Also my prerogative. I have a visa, I pay my bills, I do not deal in drugs."

She reached into the cooler for a Carta Blanca, asking me by a lift of the brow if I want one. Popping them open, she goes on, in a milder but still practical tone. "My dear, losing Mr. Raven in the desert would be child's play." She hands the beer and pats my knee. "That is not my plan. I regard Mr. Raven as a member of my party. That's why we've been waiting for him. Naturally."

Well, three days later they pull out. Arden leads the way on the resurrected Youths for Christ motorcycle, then follows the blue van, with Maurio at the wheel pulling brightly colored scarves out of his ear, and Vi beside him, throwing kisses as if they are flowers. They wave and smile, and I wave back trying to look carefree but feeling like I am about to have cardiac arrest. Oh, Ruby, Ruby, I ask myself, where will you find such high-tone chaos again?

Michael is sitting beside me on the porch, pretending to read the Guaymas newspaper. Michael can't read Spanish. He nods as they go by. Then, soon as they are out of sight, he kisses me on both cheeks and runs for his car, which he has packed up the night before. He feels smart for knowing they would leave today, though Vi made blessed sure the signals were there. But Michael does not know this. He just feels, Damn but he is one smart detective!

Now Michael is not stupid. He just hasn't paid the right kind of attention. He is about to learn now, I figure. And he is cute, as I have said.

I can see them all now, heading south on 15 toward Fresnillo—Arden, the van, and then Michael maintaining his distance.

Christ, if they were leaving today, I'd go with them! That's a fact. Nothing that good has come along these dozen years to Ruby's Campground and Trailer Park. No sir.

14

HUM

Of course I was aware throughout this odyssey of ours that back in the States hulked the insistent shadow of my Uncle Groot, his foot tapping with mounting irritation. Aunt Vi, however, felt quite secure from him. Her reasons were sometimes practical and sometimes mystical. Preferring the mystical ones, she seldom troubled explaining the practical ones. And though we were more than a decade away from the earthquake in question, I nevertheless moved from time to time in that colorless anxiety characteristic of anybody who grew up during the Eisenhower years. Also I remembered my aunt's carelessness over those bookmaking tabs not a year ago.

Carelessness is the wrong word. She put her care into devising the plan and then into serving sake to the appealing young officers. The execution of the plan had by then simply become irrelevant.

It was certainly from my aunt that I came to understand there is not much difference between a work of art and a crime. Both require a great deal of imagination on the part of the person who invents as well as on the part of the critic. Or to put it another way, my aunt's crime was completed by her arrest. The day the two young men set down their sake cups and politely accused her of bookmaking, her art had found its audience.

Not that my aunt depended for her self-definition as bookmaker on an audience. No, my aunt became a bookie the moment she decided to be one. When her decision was corroborated by the Los Angeles Police Department her delight increased immeasurably, but not her belief.

I can hear you tapping your foot, implacable as Uncle Groot. You want me to get to the point, but you are not at all sure what the point is. Something to do with parenting and fitness, you say. I will find the point for you, I who am experienced at traversing warrens, by night and by day. If you have the right to ask, then surely I have the right to answer.

It has to do with motorcycles and the death of my aunt.

I can hear you draw in your breath sharply. You assume my aunt was killed by a motorcycle. You, with your odd sense of cause and effect! No, my aunt was not killed by a motorcycle. Mine, or anybody else's. Quite the contrary.

It was my aunt, pointing into a clump of grass one morning near Guaymas, who first showed me those motorcycle parts abandoned by the Youths for Christ.

Those of you who tend to be quiet and thoughtful I would like to leave right here for the time being, following my aunt's gaze into the patch of grass springing through strewn motorcycle parts.

The rest can come with me. You are upset about the motorcycle. Or maybe motorcycles in general upset you, and the thought of a woman on a motorcycle, especially when she is not a mannequin passenger, drives you wild. Step to the rear of the bike, please.

Well, part of your problem is that you are thinking about men on motorcycles. You are thinking of arrogant noise and sideways leers through tinted face shields. You are thinking of sprawling legs and phallic innuendo.

Motorcycles do not need to be noisy. They can hum. The hum means they are well cared for and do not require your attention. And the rider does not require your attention. The rider's attention is elsewhere.

The rider is watching for wild flowers. She is feeling the ripple of asphalt, feeling for the bank of a curve, listening for the bird call or the thunk of manhole cover. She is with things, as things. She is reaching, at odd moments, for what they stand for. Between her and the wind there is nothing but her own calm mind.

Now you may be ready to join the others, those we left staring into the grass at the abandoned motorcycle parts. You may both have come to the conclusion that a motorcycle was absolutely essential to my becoming a poet.

That much was true and it was powerful. But there was something more to be gained from contemplating those motorcycle parts, something that eluded me because I was a trifle impetuous in those days and thought in terms of single meanings, a habit that the young poet was obliged, in time, to discard.

But I am getting ahead of myself. Let us just say it is mid-July of the year in question (I refer to the alleged abduction), and that my Aunt Vi—archaeologist of the bizarre—is pointing into a pile of motorcycle parts, with Ruby on her left and me on her right.

Now Ruby is the owner of the campground where we are staying. She is not much younger than my aunt and is a retired hooker, from what I can gather, and I am more than a little in love with her. Probably you feel shocked. That suits me fine, but if you would like to understand the state of my heart, remember what I said about the difference between a man on a motorcycle and a woman. I am talking about love without the leer through tinted windshield.

Anyway, we had been at Ruby's a couple of weeks and though Aunt Vi was eager to get on to Guanajuato, she kept delaying our departure. When I asked about it she quoted the I Ching. Something like, Fox who crosses the great frozen waters gets tail wet. Finally I figured out she was afraid we might lose the private investigator who had followed us from L.A. This puzzled me, but Aunt Vi, I was discovering, knew what she was doing. Besides, I needed more quiet mornings when over coffee and mangoes Ruby spread her wisdom before me. I thought that, like Aunt Vi with her weight lifting, I was growing stronger.

At last the color in Michael Raven's face changed from green to pale rose. As soon as he could walk, he followed us around writing things down in a small notebook, believing we could not see him. We began to pack. Michael walked out onto the sea wall with a fishing pole and watched through binoculars, tiny binoculars that folded as slim as a cigarette case, until—in a characteristic moment of clumsiness—he dropped them into the Gulf. My friend Ramón dove for them all afternoon without success.

Ruby cried a little into my braids as we said good-bye next morning. But I felt blessed and good. Michael sat in a wicker chair on Ruby's porch, pretending to read the morning paper. I walked close past him so that if he wanted to say something he could, but it was too soon for that. He just grunted and shook his paper into obedience.

Maurio (the man mentioned as my accomplice) was at the wheel of the van, trying to negotiate some parting magic trick and getting himself tangled up in scarves. At his side was Aunt Vi, who called to me in a voice unnecessarily penetrating, "We'll try to make it to Mazatlán, dear, for one last night on the sea."

Then she looked over at dear Ruby, gave her a wink, nodded at Maurio to start the engine, looked pleased with herself, with Michael and with Ramón, who was patting her arm, pleased with us all. I crossed over to the motorcycle that Ramón and I had created from the pile of parts in the weeds and gave her a gentle kick. She started a little ragged, then with a gentle rev, fell into a hum. We bumped slowly toward the highway, and Michael stole a glance over his paper just as Maurio began pulling a bright parade of flags from his left ear.

15

REARVIEW MIRROR

It was not until the next day, some miles out of Durango, that I noticed Michael was no longer following. I pulled over to the side, signaling to Maurio, who came careening up beside me on the shoulder of the highway. I suggested a search party, but Maurio was tired and noncommittal. Aunt Vi, he explained, was lying down in the van, resting. I climbed into Maurio's seat for a better look at her. She was very still. I hardly breathed, thinking, That is how she will look. Suddenly she opened her eyes, improbably alert.

"We'll wait for him in Fresnillo," she said, as if answering.

But I had not asked.

In town we chose a hotel right on 15 so that Michael would spot the van on his way in. We were all exhausted and hardly spoke through dinner. Maurio insisted on sleeping in the van. We saw him safely locked in, then went to our small room overlooking the road. It was very quiet all night, and dark too, except when now and then headlights floated across the pink stucco ceiling.

The next morning Aunt Vi was sitting up in bed, writing energetically. She had an idea for her novel. With a lilt of her eyelashes, she declared herself inspired. Apparently her concern for Michael had dodged down some corridor of her mind.

I learned something else about art that day. The person who is pursuing art (or perhaps the person pursued by art) has to be given a twenty-four-hour pass while others make decisions, judgments, sandwiches, and wrong turns. Maurio was not much help for the same reason my aunt was not much help. Oh, he drove the van well enough, but opinions were beyond him. I felt a little pissed, as people do in such situations, especially when I realized we had missed the road south to Guanajuato and for the last fifty miles had been traveling east to Tampico.

It was late afternoon when I made that discovery. I pulled off at a cantina, so I could study the map in a real chair. Maurio pulled off just behind, and we asked the young man throwing knives into the dirt to put gas in the van.

Walking into that cantina was like being in a John Wayne movie where everybody pauses, whiskey glasses poised, and the piano player freezes over his keys. To tell you the truth, neither Maurio nor my aunt noticed, they were so absorbed. I did not like my own self-consciousness a bit, so I sort of shuffled my feet, nodded toward the gawking barflies, called for a Carta Blanca, and bent officiously over my map. In that moment I was agreeing to take charge.

I led my dear somnambulists back toward San Luís, where the fatal error had been made. The sun was just dripping down behind the flying cactuses and jackrabbits. In my rearview mirror the windshield of the van flashed the sun, then it cleared and for a moment I could see Maurio bend toward my aunt, could see their heads come close, then disappear in the next flash of sun.

We had dinner in town, then camped just south on 57 with our noses in the right direction for an early start. It was cold that high up. Mountain cold. I lay in my sleeping bag on the roof of the van, watching those stars in their star-spins, thinking about art and poets and magic, thinking about Michael Raven alone somewhere.

In the morning I heard a crackling sound and hung my head over the side. There was Aunt Vi, always the first to rise, crossing and recrossing the tiny field, throwing a handful of twigs on the fire, then leaving at a new angle, returning with more twigs, moving as if in some ancient dance, her leopard-skin robe flapping and billowing in the chill breeze.

"Morning," I called to her in my sleepy voice.

She looked up from the fire. "Ah, the Queen of Cups." And she bowed in my direction.

I threw her down a kiss.

It was not far to Guanajuato, less than a hundred fifty miles. Aunt Vi had promised a castle, and as we wound through the mountains I wondered if it would be a castle that only she could see, or whether we all might expect bed and board there. My own need of a castle was particularly acute at the time, but I was trying to fortify myself against disappointment. Nevertheless, as we rose through the village, my expectations escaped out from under their lid. And suddenly, there it was, El Castillo de Guanajuato.

It was beautifully preserved, four hundred years old if it was a day. I got the feeling that the same people had lived in it always, mending roofs, replacing downspouts, adding plumbing, renovating the kitchen, until here they were, four hundred years later, and home was still home, having held the line against time and decay. There was even a television set in the lobby.

We each had our own room, very fine ones they were too, with red velvet drapes and bedspreads, tile floors, stone fireplaces, and a panorama of the village below, mountains beyond. Ours were the last three rooms in the house, as the bellhop told us, because a busload of American school teachers was expected in late afternoon.

We retreated alone into our rooms, I think in a need none of us was aware of until satisfaction became possible. For nearly three weeks we had been a band of gypsies, and now we would be a household of royalty. There was a richness and comradeship in either arrangement, but for now, the royalty appealed—with its fringe benefits of a real bed, a fireplace, and a bathtub just down the hall.

The fire was already laid, so I threw in a match, partly to take the chill off the room but mostly just for the joy of it. Then I wandered off in search of that bathtub. Somebody had left a box of Mickey Mouse bubble bath behind, so I shook in too much and filled the tub up to the top. I floated and dreamed until the water got chill, then I ran down the hall, leaving little puddles behind. The fire was almost out, so I blew it aflame and put on more wood. Then I crawled between clean sheets and fell asleep.

It was on the terrace at dinner that Michael Raven finally appeared. He was sitting at a corner table by himself, reading a guidebook, or rather pretending to. He was wearing the same murky drip-dry suit and was gone green in the face again. He had tucked the white linen napkin carefully over his filthy shirt front. I tried without success to catch his eye until Aunt Vi spotted him, and called gaily, "Ooeee, Michael. Over here!"

Michael dove down behind his guidebook, while the entire busload of American teachers looked in his direction. Just then his arroz con pollo arrived. I managed to restrain Aunt Vi through his dinner, which he ate hurriedly behind a barrier of disheveled road maps. When at last the waiter settled his flan in front of him, Aunt Vi, unable to restrain herself a moment longer, lurched into motion across the terrace. Michael bolted into the bushes. Aunt Vi was undaunted, however, and assured me at bedtime that Michael would accompany us tomorrow on our visit to the mummies.

I was surprised on both accounts. My plans did not include mummies, nor, I suspected, did Michael's. Nevertheless, next morning we were both dutifully lined up outside the iron staircase leading down into the catacombs.

Aunt Vi stood first on one foot, then the other, clacked her canes together, and tossed her head impatiently, while the guide explained the local embalming techniques and showed clippings from a tattered *National Geographic,* twin to the one my aunt had spread before me at the Thousand Oaks Rest Home two months before.

Michael was at the outer rim of the gaggle of teachers, leaning incongruously against a small pine, as if for support, while one particularly animated lady held a crumpled map under his nose, over which she gestured, cooed, and grimaced by turn. Michael's eyes were fixed on Aunt Vi, however, and Aunt Vi's eyes were fixed on those iron stairs.

The guide had issued various directives for safe descent, to which my aunt paid not the least attention. The formidable staircase wound downward in circles, probably a hundred and fifty feet. It was quite a trick getting in line ahead of Aunt Vi, but I managed, and nodded to Maurio to follow behind. That way we had her sandwiched in. As I stood at the head of the stairs a hot blast of air assaulted my face, as if from some ancient subterranean beast whose irritation had been fermenting since the days of Quetzalcoatl. From behind I could feel my aunt's soft insistence. She must move forward. So I kept going, deliberately slowing her as we eased into darkness, sliding both hands down the cold bannister, ready to brace at any moment.

Finally I felt dirt beneath my foot. I led Aunt Vi off a ways from the staircase, and we stood quietly, blindly, listening to the others murmur down like an underground waterfall. The guide shouted something in a tone that seemed inappropriately shrill, like a Mexican master of ceremonies announcing the next act. A string of light bulbs along either side of the cave went on then, and I could see people lounging against the walls, people who had not come with us down the staircase.

Aunt Vi let out a low exclamation of appreciation. It was then I realized these were the mummies. They were all clothed, as if for a party. Grandmothers in black linen, soldiers in obscure ornamental uniforms, girls in muslin frocks, boys in tight little antique suits, ladies in floor-length gowns. Everybody stood, most of them in relaxed postures, as if they might lean suddenly forward and introduce themselves or offer a canapé.

Finally the schoolteachers began to talk, there was a laugh or two, people began to breathe. The guide led us past the loungers along the wall, down another dim branch of the cave. People broke into little groups. Some walked arm in arm. I couldn't see Michael. Maurio stayed close to Aunt Vi.

We stopped at what looked like the entrance to another corridor. A second theatrical flash of light revealed a pile of bones so high it curved just beneath the dirt ceiling. Not a mix of bones and not dirty bones. The mountain before us was composed of pure white femurs, neatly stacked, and extending back into the cave over a hundred feet, the guide explained. Next we saw a stack of pelvic bones. By the time we got to the skulls I was pretty much innured, but apparently Michael was not. In the burst of electric light I saw him lean toward the mountain of skulls, lurch back, and then lean forward again.

Before I realized that it was blackout time again, Maurio was on his way for the catch, characteristically just a little too late. Michael had already grazed a skull with his foot, and the avalanche had begun. The schoolteachers broke into a run, the guide screaming high-pitched directions. I grabbed Aunt Vi and Maurio grabbed Michael. We dragged them back, while three million skulls broke loose, bounding, crashing, and rolling down, thundering like the devil's own bowling alley.

Nobody was hurt. People tend to survive the larger calamities, preferring to die from trifles. *Preferring* is the wrong word. Actually, most people—given the choice—probably would prefer to die under an avalanche of skulls than in their own sweet beds. However, the avalanche carries with it a roar calculated to put one on one's guard. You get determined, feeling maybe that the cosmos is trying to put one over on you. That makes you pretty nearly invincible, not in an heroic, but in an everyday kind of way.

Now probably Michael Raven did not feel exactly invincible. Still it was clear he was feeling something on that bus ride back up the mountain. He sat next to Maurio, instead of dodging around, pretending he didn't know us. That evening at dinner he walked out on the terrace and asked if he could sit at our table. Not that he made any speeches. He just quietly joined the party to which he had belonged—according to my aunt—for several weeks.

Naturally the avalanche had its impact on her, too. Her muse, temperamental midway through the novel, accepted her place in our party as uncompromisingly as did Michael. Every morning now Aunt Vi sat out on the terrace in the sunshine, writing her gothic romance, which each morning bore a different title. A waiter named Chavo, with a face like a prizefighter, began to take an interest in her literary endeavors and would bring her cups of Twining's English breakfast tea at regular intervals, coming and going with a kind of hulking pace that charmed my aunt, without distracting her from her work.

Absorbed as she was, the rest of us wandered off into the surrounding hills, Maurio and Michael together, and me alone. I was starting to write poetry. Oh, I had written poems before. Shoe boxes of them. But these were different. They had what my Aunt Vi called, after reading several, "voice." These poems wrote themselves under trees and beside streams. They wrote themselves on napkins at dinner. There was a kind of Sorcerer's Apprentice feel to it. Poems ran in under the doors at night and rose about my sleeping head.

I think we lived like this for a month or more. But I am not sure. If anyone thought about time, nobody spoke of it. The coming and going of tourist buses every three days seemed sufficient demarcation, along with breakfast, lunch, and dinner. When Aunt Vi announced one morning she had only one more chapter to write, time called attention to itself like a digital clock in the dark.

She was out on the terrace. I was following the footpath that ran behind the terrace hedge, intending not to speak because she was obviously writing with intense concentration.

"Arden, is that you?" she called, not raising her eyes from the page.

I pushed through the hedge and climbed onto the patio. She held up her arms to me and I caught a glimpse of luminous star-eyes before she crushed me into her sweet-smelling slimness and her notebook sheets of manuscript.

"I'm about to finish," she said.

The prizefighter came up with two cups of tea, which he set out on a clean tablecloth, then flashed us a parting smile like a deserted gold mine. Then she gestured me into a chair, passed the dish of lemons absently, and sharpened her eyes down to the matter at hand. "Arden, I need to talk to you, one artist to another."

I still wasn't used to being called an artist, even though she had called me one every day for months. Being an artist seemed such a holy thing. Still, I heard her call me that long enough for it to incubate in some dark corner of my mind and finally, years later, to sprout up like Jack's beanstalk in the public thoroughfare, blocking traffic and creating a public nuisance.

Anyway, I took her request for help seriously, not just because she was my aunt, not just because she was a beloved friend, but because, while I did not yet believe I was an artist, I never doubted she was.

The problem, she said, was how to end her novel.

"Well, how do novels usually end?" I asked her.

"They end," she said, taking a sip of tea, "either in marriage or in death."

"Well?"

"That is hardly a satisfying solution. Because, my dear, life doesn't end in marriage or death. Does it?"

I started to answer, but she broke in with a wave of her hand, as if correcting her own statement. "Now it's true I've known some instances where life did end in marriage, but never," she said with an emphatic shake of her head that set the gold coins jangling about her treasure map neck, "never in death."

She spread her fingers in her lap and seemed to be studying them. Then she rubbed them, then she laughed. "I would much rather end my novel with a party. Oh, I don't mean," she went on as if anticipating an objection, "one of those stiff affairs where debts are being paid, but a party of people who belong together, celebrating. A loud, tender party," she said with satisfaction.

She got her wish. Up to a point. Michael invited Aunt Vi and me to a dinner party the next evening at the hotel. He and Maurio, he told us with some mystery, had an announcement to make. There would be a special menu, planned and served by Chavo. There was to be champagne. And, of course, a magic show.

We started with the champagne and were more than a little tight by the magic show. Maurio had borrowed Chavo's tuxedo and was supposed to look distinguished but looked rather like a clown. Michael got the latest shipment of teachers bombed on champagne, and they were making paper airplanes out of their party napkins and sailing them all over the patio. Maurio passed among the ladies, tripping over his cuffs, and pulling coins from their ears. They were delighted. By way of finale he pulled a jackrabbit from his top hat. He held it gently aloft for a moment, then set it down. It went skidding off into the shrubbery amidst thundering applause. He was beside himself with pleasure.

During hors d'oeuvres Michael kept shuffling his feet under the table, adjusting his collar, and knocking the saltcellar over. Every time he knocked the salt over, Aunt Vi would make him throw a pinch over his left shoulder. Or was it the right? Anyway, it was clear Michael was working up to his announcement. Finally he cleared his throat, knocked over the salt one last time, hastily threw a pinch over his shoulder, and began.

Now I wish I could remember what Michael Raven said because it was truly splendid. But I can't. Champagne does that to me. The configurations are all there but the details are gone. Still, if I run up on the configuration, details may follow.

He wanted us to know that improbable as it seemed he and Maurio were silly in love and very happy, wanting us to share their silliness, their happiness, and not to think it was odd or against nature or criminal or reprehensible or ungrateful.

Aunt Vi began to cry with pleasure, giving Michael a kiss and her blessing, and then a kiss for Maurio, who burst into tears. Then I burst into tears. Michael knocked over the salt. Then he knocked over the champagne. We were all laughing and mopping up champagne, and talking over their plans to go live in San Francisco and start a catering business, when a stranger came up to the table.

That is, he was a stranger to everybody but Michael, who—if he had not become so healthy in the Mexican mountains—would certainly have turned that old green of his. Michael, after a brief but unsuccessful explanation of the spilled champagne (he realized midway that he would have to begin editing his life for popular consumption), introduced the stranger to us as Luther P. Grinwall, a fellow private investigator.

Grinwall looked like a member of the SS and kept calling Michael by his last name, all the time maintaining an elaborate politeness toward Aunt Vi. For a while she did not ask him to sit down, then nodded in the direction of a chair. He sat in champagne. Aunt Vi was sorry.

Into this confusion the harpies flung yet another stranger, one following in the footsteps of Grinwall, but this time known not by Michael but by me. It was Malthus. Malthus, with a love as tenacious as poison ivy. I introduced him around the table. Grinwall, of course, he already knew. Aunt Vi invited him to join us. He sat in champagne. Aunt Vi was sorry.

Grinwall explained he was here at the request of his client, Mr. Groot, and that he was replacing Raven, as he called him. Raven had not worked out. No offense. We were all adults, he trusted. Even Raven there. And duty was simply that, duty and nothing more. No reason to bust up the little party, of course. Tomorrow soon enough to make all necessary arrangements. Mr. Groot a very patient man.

With that, Grinwall rose, his pants sticking to his fanny, and bade us all good evening. Malthus showed no such diplomacy. He wanted to chat about demography, whatever that is. Maurio and Michael excused themselves and strolled with Mona Lisa smiles toward their favorite mountain path. Aunt Vi yawned. The prizefighter brought coffee. Malthus, taking a sip, hazarded it was a blend of mocha java and Colombian supremo. Aunt Vi said she had to go to bed.

She rose from her chair, her necklaces jingling and her bracelets clacking. "I hope you realize, young man," said Aunt Vi, gesturing with the handle of her cane, "that both Arden and I are committed to our course. You'll not find us easily moved for your whims—but for our own we can move as quickly as gypsies. That leaves you at something of a disadvantage, by my calculation." Then she smiled with all her charm and left us alone on the terrace.

I did not sleep well that night. There was something about Malthus and his needs that I found draining. Sooner or later capitulation would begin to look attractive. Whatever he wanted always took the form of my giving up something. For my own good. Not until years later did I realize that at the center of each of Malthus's desires was a cipher. He wanted the absence of something, not its presence. It was this invisibility about his wants that made them seem superior to my own, making mine appear egoistic or even grossly material—the motorcycle, for instance, that I had wanted early in summer so that I could distress him by fracturing my skull.

In short, Malthus wanted to marry me. We needed each other. Without me, life was nothing. He wanted to be settled, to know where everything was, and to have children. The urgency of my own needs along these lines he allowed to be far greater than his own. I was headed for dissolution and madness, leading a nomadic life with a sick (not to mention crazy) old lady, whose death was both assured and imminent. My part in this event would be accounted by some as "ambiguous." For what he, Malthus, understood to be guileless irresponsibility, society might very well see as Manslaughter Two.

Have you ever had the experience of somebody picking out of the air a message intended for you? By rights I should have received that special delivery prophecy. Was I not my aunt's own niece? Was I not a poet? Was I not mostly Indian? Had I not been directed by my spiritual guide to gaze at the pile of motorcycle parts in the patch of grass?

Yes, but I had failed to see them as death emblems. That was the problem. To me they were either junk or possibility. Aunt Vi seemed to come down on the side of possibility, so I made a motorcycle out of them. But I did not see them as part of a process involving decay and creation. I only saw the creation part. Rusty as they were . . . those wheels and gears and cables . . . It had gone right by me.

So I was musing on death and motorcycles and marriage that night, pacing across the tile floor, perching on the window ledge. There was a pencil of light under the door connecting my room with Aunt Vi's. I wanted her to explain what she meant yesterday when she said novels ended either in death or marriage. I had some feeling that the novel we were in was concluding, whether we wanted it to or not, and that Malthus had arrived with the two possible conclusions in hand, like matched luggage. Death and marriage. Aunt Vi said life could end in marriage but not in death. What had she meant?

I eased the door open. Aunt Vi was sitting up in bed, pen in hand, her blue notebook open in her lap. She was looking off across the room as I had so often seen her do, evoking the next turn in her fiction. Cautiously I shut the door and crossed back to the window ledge. Sleep was by now out of the question. Besides, there was a moon, the kind that pries your eyelids open and makes you want to howl. Below, on the terrace, Chavo was stacking the last chair upside down on a table. We had kept him up, Malthus and I. But now he would go home and lie in his wife's arms, lulled by the sleep of children.

A jackrabbit hopped onto the meadow below the terrace and poised there in the moonlight as if thinking. Then I heard voices, male voices, in talk they believed was quiet, yet carried like the moonlight. The rabbit broke and ran, as Michael and Maurio made their way up the path toward the castle, their arms around each other.

I had to talk to Aunt Vi. Again I eased the door open. She was still writing, or rather thinking, in the posture of a rabbit in moonlight. This time I went in, calling to her softly. I did not know until I touched her that she was dead.

And when I bent to kiss her I knew she was not dead, but off on her travels again. Though it was not the first time she had answered a question before I asked, it would be the last.

So I cried for a while. Eventually I had some impulse to prepare her for her funeral, but when I leaned close there was the fresh and festive smell of Mickey Mouse bubble bath. I picked up her notebook, wanting still to do some small service before I would have to turn her over to Grinwall and my Uncle Groot.

I pulled a chair up to her bedside and began to read her novel. It was called *Secret of the Skulls,* and she had dedicated it "To a Young Poet." So I felt I had the go-ahead, that I was not an intruder but an invited guest.

Probably most of you know the book. It was on the gothic romance best-seller list for sixteen months and won the Moira de Vere Fiction Award for 1960. Uncle Groot made a second fortune by it, they say.

But what you probably don't know is that I wrote the last three pages. Yes. Because, you see, it wasn't finished. So instead of washing my aunt for burial, I finished writing her novel.

It was morning by then. Grinwall and Malthus were on the terrace early, having coffee and rolls. I could see them from the window. Ready now, I put my aunt's notebook back into her waiting hands. Then I went downstairs to turn myself in.

16

WITH FRIENDS LIKE THESE

My name is Allison Honey and I'm a cook for Raven and Carbonara, Caterers, San Francisco. I wasn't always a cook. I used to be a graduate student. In fact, when I first met Arden Benbow that's what I was. I worked in the reading room for graduate students. Library work.

Before that I was a research assistant but I got fired for dropping cigarette ashes into Dr. Gridley's card files. "Flicking" ashes, Dr. Gridley said. She thought I would burn up the work of a lifetime.

They are like that, academics. They think the world is holding its breath for those index cards, and that those cards are always about to go up in smoke. Or something. I knew one professor who kept his manuscripts in the refrigerator. His wife complained, but it did no good because he said refrigerators were fireproof. (He also kept twenty-dollar bills in the butter-keeper, but that is by the way.)

So I had already got fired for endangering Dr. Gridley's work of a lifetime, a point you should understand, so you won't think my troubles began and ended with Arden Benbow and her rabbits.

Actually I think I never belonged in graduate school. It's like a lot of things. I started school when I was five years old and just kept going. Besides, I liked to read. But Dr. Gridley told me I wasn't Ph.D. material. She said I was the only person she ever knew who read Henry James for the story.

I'm not an intellectual. I would never think to put my manuscripts in the refrigerator.

If I had been that kind of person, the little accident over the paper on Henry James would never have happened. So you can see it was not Arden's fault at all.

Maybe I am not making myself clear. You see, Arden had three hundred rabbits and she tried everything in the world to cut down on them because it cost a fortune to feed them and she had six kids and was divorced. Arden is a poet.

I first met her in the reading room. Well, actually I didn't formally meet her, but I noticed her. Everyone did. You see, it's always very quiet in the reading room. Only intellectuals tend to go there, and they are quiet people by nature, usually reading, or writing their thoughts down on three-by-five cards, sometimes color coded. Suddenly somebody said (right out loud), "Of course!" Actually it was more like a shout. When everybody looked at her, she just smiled back, and then went on reading.

After that I started to say hello when she came in, and sometimes we would meet in the halls and talk about one thing and another. When she heard my car hadn't been running for two months, nothing would do but she had to fix it. That's the kind of person Arden Benbow is.

She came over the next afternoon on a motorcycle, with a big toolbox lashed onto the back. Her hair was braided down her back under her white helmet, and she wore a midnight-blue leather jacket with zippers all over it, very stylish. She looked like Amelia Earhart, I thought.

"What's her name?" she asked me, lifting the hood and peering in.

"Whose?"

"Your car's."

"Oh, the car doesn't have a name."

"No wonder she won't run."

"Well, what do you suggest?"

"*You've* got to name her," she said, pulling caps off things and peering in. "Or it doesn't count."

"Dr. Gridley says I have no imagination."

"Dr. Gridley can blow it out her ear."

That one caught me off balance. I thought cars would stop on the freeway and that lights would short out all over three counties. Nothing happened. In fact I felt—you might say—peaceful.

"Shall I get us a beer?" I asked.

She raised up a little, with her braid dangling just over the carburetor and a smudge of grease on one cheek. "Bless you," sne said.

"I think her name is Toby," I called over my shoulder.

Well, after that I wanted to do something nice for Arden. I asked her to dinner at my place because cooking is one thing I really do well (I think I mentioned I am a cook for Raven and Carbonara in the Mission District). It was then she explained about the six kids, the three hundred rabbits, and her lover, Alice. The kids I already knew about, but the rabbits and the lover named Alice came as a surprise. Otherwise I would have offered right away to cook at her house instead of mine. As it was, it took a long time for me to see that as a solution and get the hour and everything worked out OK.

My boyfriend, Miller, told me that Arden Benbow was after my body. I was nervous enough without Miller's suspicion. I almost called in sick. Instead I put on more makeup than usual and wore a dress and earrings that hurt my ears. I loaded Toby up with bowls and pans and whisks, pints of cream, carrots, parsnips, celery, onions, and chuck roast for pot-au-feu. Also Julia Child.

From this point on, it is hard to say what happened. Looking back on it, I would have to say that instead of things happening in their usual one-at-a-time way, events kept running into each other, like people in an airport. If you don't understand that, you will never understand why I agreed to take the two rabbits.

Let's start outside Arden's house. It is Sunday evening, early January, and I have just pulled up with my cargo of carrots, parsnips, etcetera. My ears are tiny points of pain. I get out of the car and am opening up the trunk, when a blue Mercedes full of people pulls up and I see they are children, except of course for the driver, who is late forties. Doors start popping open and the man runs around as if to get everybody in some kind of order, but they are tearing around, falling down, flinging their coats onto the grass, skinning knees, grabbing and kissing the dog who runs out to meet them, and getting cotton candy stuck in their hair, which the dog tries to lick out.

The man, who I guess is Mr. Benbow, raises his hand in farewell as the last of them waves and disappears inside. He is rumpled, in his camel's hair suit, and looks a little helpless. From the back I can see his graying hair is combed carefully over a bald spot about the size of a silver dollar. He turns as if he can feel my eyes playing over this tender area, and flashes me a smile.

"You a friend of Arden?" he asks, as if he can't quite believe it.

I tell him yes and say a few polite things about school and this and that. He tells me about his kids and Disneyland and that I can call him Malthus—everybody does—and about the modern curse of split families. He sighs, looking a little like William Holden in *Sabrina* after he has lost Audrey Hepburn to Humphrey Bogart. There is something about sad, handsome men.

"Well," I tell him, trying for a lighter tone, "these things usually work out."

He sighs again, and stares off in the general direction of the puffs of clouds adrift in late afternoon smog. I pat his arm, and turn to pick up the chuck roast, carrots, parsnips, and celery. It is then that he gooses me. I drop the chuck roast. Near an anthill, but not in it, luckily.

There seems nothing to do but let him carry the roast to the door. He insists, brushing off eucalyptus leaves from the bruised meat package. I totter along behind in my three-inch heels, feeling confused, gripping the carrots, celery, and parsnips for dear life. I want Arden to open that door; I want William Holden to go away.

But it is not Arden who opens the door. It is the tallest, blackest man I have ever seen, wearing peach-colored leotards and glowering at Mr. Benbow.

"Jamie's throwing up, Malthus."

"Must be the stress," Mr. Benbow says thoughtfully. "You know, children from broken families . . . "

"Must be the cotton candy, Malthus," corrects the black man vehemently. "I won't have you feeding those kids junk all day. You understand me?"

"I can't see that it's any business of yours, Wilson," says Mr. Benbow, looking more alert and more dangerous.

Just then the black man notices me, balancing the carrots, onions, and parsnips. "Honey?" he asks, sounding suddenly warm and friendly. "Well, Honey. Come on in. We're expecting you." And he draws me in with one enormous hand, then takes the roast from Mr. Benbow, and closes the door in his face. "Alice and Arden are busy with the kids. Come on in the kitchen."

We set everything down on the counter. "I'm Wilson Topaz and that's old Earl, a friend of the family," he said, nodding toward a gentleman with a kind face, a bow tie, and a beer belly. Earl was making drinks in the blender. Would I care to try his own special recipe? He called it blueberry fizz. Made with fresh blueberries. But there was plain Scotch if I'd rather, or gin, or bourbon. What was my pleasure?

I said I'd try the blueberry fizz. Mr. Topaz made a face behind Earl's back and got caught. They both laughed, and then Mr. Topaz told me to stop calling him Mr. Topaz, that it made him feel portly and that his friends always just called him Topaz.

We all washed the vegetables. I opened Julia Child to pot-au-feu. She said to tie string around the roast and the chicken for easy removal, but I had forgotten to get any chicken.

"Oh, well," said Earl, who was pretty far along in blueberry fizz. "Probably never notice." Then he yelled, "Anybody got some string?"

"On my kite," called a faraway voice. Then there was barking.

"Jamie," said Earl with a satisfied expression. "That'll be Jamie."

"She got sick again on that amusement park shit Malthus feeds them," Topaz said, scraping the carrots vindictively.

Just then a girl came in wearing a flannel shirt and blue jeans, carrying a yellow kite with eyes painted on it. "Hi. I threw up. You must be Honey. You look like honey. Why you want the string?" She stuck an experimental finger into Earl's blender.

From that point on the recipe for pot-au-feu became mixed up with all those kids. One minute I was peeling and quartering turnips and the next I would be reading *Winnie the Pooh*. It was crazy. There were four grown-ups in the house and we weren't quite enough, I thought. Topaz said that however many there were was however many were needed. The Topaz Principle, he called it. By seven o'clock the pot-au-feu still had an hour and a half to go, so Alice cooked the kids hot dogs over the barbecue.

I liked Alice. She was on the small side, with feathery short hair going gray, and she walked a little like a dancer, but not exactly. If you could put together a sailor and a ballet dancer, you might have an idea of Alice's walk. It was graceful but strong. She couldn't have been over five three in her stocking feet.

Finally the last kid was in bed and I realized when the Old English sheepdog had run through after the calico cat and knocked Julia Child on the floor that what had started off as pot-au-feu had most certainly ended up as boeuf Bourguignon.

"So be it," said Alice, lighting the candles.

Well, it was a pretty good meal, considering. They all thought it was a whole lot better than it really was, and kept saying so. Earl would nod every few bites and say, "My compliments to the chef." Afterwards we had coffee and Alice played the piano. It was a soft kind of tune. I thought Alice might be about to cry, but then she looked up from her music and smiled at me. Brandy makes me feel like that, like her smile did.

Next Topaz picked up a saltshaker and sprinkled salt on the floor, looking at Arden. She smiled at him and stood up on the salt and started sliding her feet around in a shush-shush kind of way that fell into a pattern at last, or it had been there all the time. I felt held and then set down.

Earl got up to do the dishes. Then the Old English sheepdog came in with another dog and they licked the salt up off the floor. I felt like if I didn't get up and go home now I never would. Arden said she wanted to show me something first. We wrapped up the leftover carrots, parsnips, and beef. Then Arden led me back into the living room and over to the mantel, where there was a shoe box. Inside were two tiny bunnies with fat ears. I really do not know what came over me. I had to have those bunnies. I was not forced into taking them, as Miller insists.

So it was not Arden's fault when Isabel Archer and Madame Merle ate my seminar paper on Henry James. Rabbits are smarter than you might think. I can tell you a story about mine that would convince you.

I don't know whether I mentioned this, but I used to live in the part of West L.A. called Little China, just off Sautelle Boulevard. In fact, the Chinese market was just opposite my duplex. So I ate fortune cookies as a habit. Every morning at the breakfast table I would set out two fortune cookies. I would break the first one in half, read the fortune aloud, give it to Isabel, and eat the cookie. Then I would break the second cookie, read Madame Merle her fortune, and hand it over. I tried at first feeding them the cookie but they preferred eating the fortunes, so it worked out fine for everybody.

Well, one morning I broke open Isabel's cookie and read her the advice, "Beware of flatterers." She hopped off with the fortune in her mouth, saving it for later. I read Madame Merle hers. It said, "Opportunity exists for he who seizes it." She ate her fortune, wiggling her nose, the two ends of the paper gradually disappearing toward the middle. Then she hopped over to Isabel, nuzzled her affectionately, whipped her fortune out of her mouth, and ate it up.

See what I mean? So it was no accident they ate my seminar paper on Henry James.

Because in her way Dr. Gridley had been right all along. I was no scholar. Even though I knew that's where they belonged, I never kept manuscripts in the refrigerator. After I had given Isabel and Madame Merle their fortunes all those months, they eventually gave me mine, which was to be a cook for Raven and Carbonara, Caterers. And thanks to Arden Benbow, who found me my job and who knows more about rabbits and fortunes than anybody.

17

A GEOLOGICAL ASIDE

May 23, 1972

Nobody ever died of rippling ground. People die when buildings hit them on the head. You can laugh condescendingly at Indians and their superstitions, but who ever heard of an Indian being buried alive under a tepee? So first I'm going to tell you what the Indians thought earthquakes were and then I'll give you the gospel according to Cal Tech.

They saw the earth balanced on the back of a moving tortoise. Every time that tortoise took a step, the earth rocked and slid. Now whatever else I say about earthquakes, don't let that picture slip from your mind. I tell my students to put their science right on top of that tortoise and they can't go wrong.

Now earthquakes happen for a lot of reasons. One is continental drift, and it means that millions of years ago large chunks of continents detached, floated around, and crashed into land masses. We are still experiencing the impact.

Another thing is Chandler Wobble. It means the earth doesn't rotate smoothly on its axis because we bulge out at the equator. So the wobble can cause quakes, and then in turn the quakes can produce more wobble.

And then sun spots and other solar activity have an impact on earth movement, but that's a little out of my line. My own specialty is plate techtonics. When you've got two or three masses of earth traveling in different directions, then get ready for an earthquake.

The elastic rebound theory explains what happens. Wherever these plates meet, tremendous pressure builds up. These areas of intense pressure are what we call faultlines. Sometimes they relieve themselves by earth creep, where they just slide on by, half an inch a year. In other places, though, they get stuck. That's called "stick-slip." Then the pressure really builds up, and it goes on building up, until something gives—suddenly. We don't know when something will give, only that it has to, and that it's just waiting for something to trigger it. Locked plates may stay locked for a million years but eventually they crash their way out, leaving a ragged, awesome landscape. Earthquakes are dynamic reactions against prolonged inactivity.

Now California is seismically interesting because we're talking about thirty million years of plate techtonics, and it's not over yet. California has usually one quake a year that causes damage, but many more that go completely unnoticed by most people. That's because they're not paying attention. They like to think the earth is a finished product, while there's really no such thing.

Earthquakes remind us. The major reminders in this century of course begin with the San Francisco quake in 1906 (Richter 8.3), the Long Beach quake in 1933 (6.3), the Imperial Valley shock in 1940 (7.1), the Kern County quake in 1952 (7.7), and the San Fernando quake in 1971 (6.6).

It's this last you're interested in and the San Andreas Fault. But it makes no sense to talk about the San Andreas in isolation, because that fault is only one of ten significant faults in California, all part of a worldwide system. No techtonic action is an isolated event.

Now the San Andreas is about six hundred fifty miles long and probably extends into the earth to a depth of somewhere between twenty and thirty feet. From San Francisco to the Gulf of California its course is mainly northwest-southeast. But right at the San Bernardino Mountains it jogs a pretty true east-to-west direction. This hitch is called the "big bend," and it's where the Pacific Plate is trying to get north around the mountains and has run full tilt into the North American Plate. This is a classic stick-slip situation, a locking that is a symptom of continental drift.

Of course, some of this pressure is eased by earth creep, at the rate of anywhere from half an inch to two and a half inches a year. But from Banning to Cholame the fault is locked tight. And I would say that was the source of the San Fernando quake you asked me about.

This quake occurred on February 9, 1971, at forty-seven seconds after 6:00 A.M. Luckily. If it had happened an hour or two later, a whole lot more people would have died than the fifty-eight that did. The quake lasted twelve seconds, but of course it felt a lot longer to the people anywhere near the epicenter. And a number of strong aftershocks occurred during the day and into the night, gradually easing over the next several weeks.

Now as quakes go, this one doesn't sound like much unless you lived through it or unless you know how to interpret the data. On the Richter scale it recorded a 6.6 (the San Francisco quake was 8.3 and the differences are logarithmic). On the Mercalli scale it rated VII or IX. You could call it moderately severe and be done. But what was unique about this quake was the strong ground motion.

Ground waves came from two different directions at once. That's called acceleration, and a 0.5 g is pretty bad. This quake rated between 0.7 g and 1.0 g. Everybody interviewed afterward mentioned the waves, and I think they scared most people more than the roar of the quake and more than actual structural damage.

Another thing about this quake that ought to be mentioned is the near disaster at the Van Norman Dam. Most dams in California were ori originally dirt construction, not necessarily the safest but certainly the cheapest. Gradually these were being replaced, and the Van Norman was already scheduled for phasing out. When the quake hit, the walls of the dam fell away to within five feet of the water line.

We are talking about a dam that could go at any moment, that was subjected to severe aftershocks, and that was situated so that eighty thousand people were directly in the path of eleven million tons of water. These eighty thousand people were evacuated quickly and efficiently, while the dam was gradually drained into a reservoir by the Army Corps of Engineers.

Now the dam keeper has been praised, the army has been praised, and Civil Defense has been praised. But I would like to honor the people who were thrown out of bed at six, and who several hours later moved quietly into the hills and waited.

So that's the fault in a nutshell. I have tried to give you the science of the thing, and remind you at the same time about the earth riding on the back of a moving tortoise. Like the Indians, people today who live along a faultline have an intimate relationship with the earth. When she speaks, they listen.

Sincerely,

Max Kasirian, Ph.D.
Department of Geophysics
California Institute of Technology

18

ALICE IN LOVE

Because my father did not believe in them, I was given no middle
name. He believed distinctions should be earned, not conferred, although
as a member of an old and fairly wealthy Boston family all his distinc-
tions had been conferred at birth by his father and he had not thought
fit ever to refuse them. Sometimes people who have never struggled be-
lieve in struggle a good deal more than those who have known struggle
from the cradle.

Having no middle name I was free to make them up. For dancing
class especially they seemed essential. I was Alice Renée Maybury for
two years, then—when I changed studios after mother's misunderstanding
with Madame Celeste—I became Alice Marie, and later Alice Louise. I
rather looked forward to my mother's altercations with my dance teachers
because they always held out the promise of a new name.

I was rather a shy child, which irritated my father, who always said
my mother and her passion for ballet were responsible for this unattrac-
tive characteristic. When he demanded I take public speaking lessons, my
mother struck a compromise by adding tap lessons to my dance reper-
toire. Since this decision coincided with my transfer to a new dance
school, I became Alice Jeanene Maybury and took to chewing gum and
painting my nails.

By now I was an adolescent, rather undersized, with a bad complexion,
and a tendency to avoid my parents at all costs. Although my family was

not Catholic, I was sent to a Catholic high school, where I was taught to play rugby and to manipulate those in power. I did very well in school, particularly in mathematics and music. In my senior year I fell in love with Al Capone and Sister Mary Joseph, the school librarian. Since both were passionate lovers of opera, I became a passionate lover of opera, and though Al Capone and Sister Mary Joseph both passed out of my life, opera never did.

My father thought opera as unhealthy as ballet and sent me to a ski resort in Switzerland, where I broke both my legs. When I started Radcliffe in the fall, I had spent three months in or on my bed reading Proust and had decided to devote my life to literature. I walked with a cane. Although this handicap was not permanent, by now I seemed a total failure to my father. It was clear I never would be any taller than five feet three inches and that all those ballet lessons had done me real and evident harm.

Nor was there a young man. My mother believed the fault lay in the design of what she called my foundation garments. That summer she spent vast sums on one wired bra after another. Next Christmas I brought Chowder home to meet my parents.

Chowder Wicks was a clumsy young man of good family whom I met in American Literature to the Civil War. Because he was on the varsity crew team and was overworked by the B-School, he had no time to read *Moby Dick*. I told him stories from Hawthorne, Poe, and Melville, while he helped me in a program of leg exercises. By Christmas, he had a "B" in American Literature to the Civil War and I walked without a limp. In the spring I taught him to dance, and he taught me to sail. By midsummer I was pregnant. The apparently endless chain of lessons that was my childhood had come to an end.

Chowder, because he loved me and because he had been raised with a belief in "doing the right thing," offered marriage. My mother and father accepted his proposal, while I declined, outlining plans for having the baby alone and going off with it to Africa where I would work with Margaret Mead.

In those days it was expected that a Radcliffe woman would speak with determination and equally well understood she would ultimately do as she was directed. We married quietly, and after honeymooning two weeks in Vermont, we returned to the home of Chowder's parents, where an apartment over the carriage house had hurriedly been prepared for us.

Chowder returned to the university for his senior year, while I retired to the little sun deck off the living room, propped my feet up on the tree-lined railing, and began rereading Proust. In my fourth month I took up the coronet, as a kind of amusement, but in my fifth month I lost my wind and by the sixth I had lost the baby as well, along with crucial parts of my reproductive system. I was twenty. I had not wanted a baby, but now that I had lost it I felt an anger so elemental it was like part of my teeth and my marrow. My mind sent off a gnashing and sparking that bit and burned others and myself and turned the light in my eyes to something new, something that made people uncomfortable.

Going to California was not my idea. It may have been nobody's idea at all, but one of those major life decisions that gets made while the house and everybody in it sleeps. And in fact I was a somnambulist. It seemed I had married because of the baby, and then there being no baby, the marriage sort of hung in mid-air. But it did not fall.

Chowder is, you see, fundamentally and consistently kind. There had been no romance, but romance by now seemed a quality that only Doris Day and Howard Keel had the remotest chance of finding, or like silk-worms, manufacturing out of their own secretions. I had nothing to complain of.

We traveled by train treating ourselves like invalids, enjoying the sun and enjoying the West opening before us. Moving slowly as we did, there was time for my sense of life to overtake me and remind me this moment was real, as real as the sun falling on my hand through the train window. But I did not feel twenty-one and I did not believe my name was Alice Maybury Wicks. Somehow the names I had fashioned for dancing school all those years seemed more authentic than the one at last bestowed by the state of Massachusetts and confirmed by the monogrammed linen handkerchiefs my Aunt Rosamund had given me hastily at the station.

Chowder went to work for the Department of Water and Power. I had some impulse to work, myself, but Chowder felt it would make him look bad to his friends at W & P. This was in the days when an idle wife was a sign of success. So I took piano lessons and dug crabgrass out of the yard.

I did that as long as I could, then I began sneaking off to play piano three times a week at a local bar. Chowder suspected infidelity and in a way he was right. Eventually I confessed and invited him to come hear me play.

Chowder sat among the patrons, unbending, poised like an oarsman listening for the starting shot. It was not a sleazy bar, nor a sinister one, nor was it dirty or even particularly noisy. Still the fact remained that Chowder was horrified. Without knowing why, he was horrified. Poor man, the first mature infusion of Bostonian pride was coursing through his arteries. And it was not to be the last.

By way of compromise, I got a job as a technical writer for Lindsey Snelling and Sons, a large engineering firm by Westlake Park, where daily I fed my lunch to the ducks and read Anthony Trollope by installment. The pay was poor, but at the time I knew very little about technical writing. When I quit last September my own tally showed I exploited them for the first ten years and they exploited me for the last ten. I was the highest ranked technical writer and the lowest paid, because I had no engineering degree, in fact no degree at all.

For twenty years Chowder and I performed the dance of the successful couple. We moved from modest apartment to modest duplex to luxury apartment to modest home to luxury home in Sherman Oaks, built on a hillside (held in place by ice plants) with an exciting view of the valley, especially by night. Chowder climbed the professional ladders set before him, remained generous, lost some hair, played handball twice a week, cheered on the Hollywood Stars and later the Los Angeles Dodgers.

A contented person does not miss joy. Not consciously, anyway. With Chowder I had a deep but limited friendship. It had grown like a healthy plant in a small pot, roots winding in intricate but confused configurations.

I met Arden Benbow nearly three years ago, when a reorganization of the department left Chowder in charge of the City Planning Division, where Malthus, her husband, was second in command and I gather had hoped to be first. To put everyone at their ease Chowder wanted to have the division—along with some old friends from the department—over for drinks out on the deck. All that day, as I baked the ham and the turkey, filled bowls with olives, peeled carrots, made guacamole, I nursed a vague anxiety about Mrs. Malthus. As I invented her, she was short and over-weight, rather pale, grasping where her husband's career was concerned. She read the *Ladies Home Journal* faithfully and snipped coupons from *Family Circle*. There were, I knew, five children. They drank powdered milk mixed each night by Mrs. Malthus, who—though she made all her own clothes—kept a private cache of Mrs. See's best chocolates, from which she nibbled in secret throughout the day. She would be angry that

Chowder had overreached her husband and at some pains to conceal her proprietary, tribal feelings.

It would be tedious. At forty-one I simply felt I could no longer respond to anyone on those terms, even if she was a guest in my house.

Of course by the time the party was well under way I forgot Mrs. Malthus and her grievance. For there is a magic in all parties, or incipient magic anyway, a sense of possibility that—despite a thousand disappoint-ments—can revive itself for one more evening. Chowder had strung Japanese lanterns along the deck, and they glowed and swung gently over the heads of these people, assembled in the name of possibility.

Some time during the evening a few people asked me to play the piano. I was glad to do it, although my shyness always makes me catch my breath a moment when I sit down to play. But I believe in people entertaining one another. Life to me is a kind of air raid going on outside and overhead. Huddled together as we are in this shuddering room, with debris raining down on our heads from time to time, those of us who can should pull from our pockets our harmonicas and play our friends into solace or sleep.

A little Gershwin, a little Cole Porter. People talking, laughing. I wasn't offended. It reminded me of my days at the piano bar all those years ago, when no one seemed to listen, except a drunk or two, with their awesome intensity. But I could feel my music enter the talking, laughing, drinking people and it was enough. I finished with a medley of "Easy to Love" and "I Can't Get Started with You."

Then there was applause, a few people murmuring their way out the door, others pouring drinks. I went into the kitchen for more tonic, turned, just as someone said, "You must be Alice."

I felt a little discharge of electricity go off—a feeling I explained to myself then as surprise, surprise that Arden was not at all as I had in-vented her. Rather than short, she was tall, with long dark hair falling free, making her look a girl, though not girlish. She had a handsome nose with a nice curve in it that she must have been teased horribly for as a child and that she must have suffered over as an adolescent. Her brown eyes, a shade too close together, seemed to balance and justify the nose, and her wide mouth with its warm smile made the whole face seem dear and cherished in an instant.

"I heard you play," she said, taking my hand in greeting. "I slipped in . . . well, if I can slip in anywhere these days." She laughed and glanced down at her belly, and for the first time I noticed she was pregnant.

I think I must have started expressing my sympathy, but she waved it away, and then a man came up who looked rather like William Holden, though not so mellow, and introduced himself as Malthus, apologized for their lateness—a baby with a rash, or some such—then steered Arden off in the direction of Chowder. It was an inauspicious beginning, but a beginning all the same.

For the next two years we met only at parties and company picnics and such, always in a group, always saying we would like to see more of one another and meaning it, but never managing to cut past the intricate pattern of family and work. It seemed as though our relationship was destined to remain potential, particularly because in the fall Arden began graduate school.

Things would have gone on in this quietly disappointing way as long as there was no slip, no shock to fling us out of the ways of custom and into the ways of innovation and creation. But of course there was a faultline under our feet.

It happened a year ago last February. Chowder and half his office had flown that morning to Chicago, where once a year they attended a four-day national convention of city planners. I was looking forward to the time alone. That night I stopped at the A & P and picked up a perfect delmonico, then to the liquor store for a split of champagne. I decided to buy one for each night. Then, because they were on sale, I had them put a case in my trunk. And some Presto Logs.

The weather was chill and dry, but not really cold. I decided to cook outside on the hibachi. The champagne was room temperature, so I opened one bottle and poured it over ice, then put two more in the refrigerator and slid the case into the pantry. I felt a deep pleasure in all these preparations. They seemed to spring equally from deliberation and carelessness. I put on some old corduroy hiking pants, my slippers, and a windbreaker. Out on the deck I pulled my favorite rattan chair up to the hibachi and stacked the charcoal in a pattern on top of the morning's crumpled *Times*. While the fire burned down, I sipped my champagne and watched the stars watching the city. Why wouldn't they throw us a message in a bottle?

I fanned the fire with a Ping-Pong paddle and opened another bottle of champagne. Then I made watercress salad with tomatoes, and chervil dressing. The fire was ready, so I cooked the steak quickly on each side, then sat down at the picnic table and enjoyed my feast, while city and stars exchanged their glances.

Instead of sleeping in the bedroom, I decided to sleep in my music room, where there was a small fireplace, a daybed, and a sliding glass door onto the deck, where the stars should not be shut out. I put on a Mozart concerto and built a fire out of kindling and Presto Logs, then did a little work from the office, sitting up in bed. Finally I turned off the stereo, set the fire screen in place, and went to sleep.

It was the roar that woke me, followed by shattering glass, and my bed trembling and creaking beneath me. At first I thought it was a nuclear blast, that the end at last was here. Then I knew it for earthquake.

I grabbed my robe and ran toward the kitchen, staggering as I went, then drew up at the kitchen door. The cupboards were all open and a-swing, while stacks of plates and bowls slid off their shelves and shattered on the kitchen tiles. I headed on to the living room and out the front door, staggering first in the doorjamb, which moved into my path.

Outside it was still pitch dark, but I could see in faint outlines my neighbors, like me, heading for the street and open space. As I ran downhill, pavement rippled under my bare feet and rolled too from an opposite direction, making me lurch in my flight, and finally fall. It was far enough.

As the neighbor children arrived I tucked the smallest under my robe, and let the others huddle around me until their parents arrived. Finally the roaring stopped, and then the shuddering. We talked in stunned tones, trying to disperse our fear into the shared atmosphere of disaster.

In the kitchen least in shambles we swallowed bitter coffee and listened to the news, each retelling the morning's experience—the yank into consciousness, the grasping for explanation, the horror of power released. A hospital had collapsed, freeways had fallen, the dam was cracked. People were dead.

I went home, fragmented as my own kitchen. Everywhere were shards of glass and debris. I scraped a place to sit on the couch and sank down. A cat climbed in through a hole in the glass door and made its way delicately across the living room to where I sat. She rubbed against my legs, and I bent to stroke her. Just as my hand touched fur, there was a boom and the world swayed. A surviving lamp fell onto the rug without breaking. I clutched the cat, while her claws dug through my bathrobe into my thighs. Aftershock. The radio had warned there would be movement as the earth settled into new configurations. Violent movement.

The cat jumped down and shook herself. I went off to the kitchen to find her some milk. The refrigerator gaped and oozed currents of catsup, mustard, milk, sour cream, and leftover chocolate mousse. I closed the refrigerator on its disarray and instead opened a tin of smoked oysters from the clutter on the floor.

I heard a tapping sound but was so disoriented I did not at first recognize it for the social signal it was. Finally I opened the kitchen door against the debris. No one there. Then I heard the sound again from a new direction and children laughing. It was the front door, and Arden was there—I knew—even before I saw her. She was leaning beside the door with Ellen on her hip and Max by the hand, while her oldest, Kip, spread arms protectingly around the other three.

"We've been evacuated. The dam."

I took the baby from her and led them all inside, in the direction of the guest room. Not much breakage there. We pushed wide the beds for play area now and sleeping later. Kip brought pillow slips they had hastily stuffed with clothes and a few prized toys, and he and Jamie got the younger children playing, while I led Arden off to the music room for some rest.

She was pale and quiet. I smoothed out my bed and settled her on it, letting down the bamboo shade to darken the room. As I moved quietly toward the door, she flung out a weary hand. I took it, welcoming that pressure of friendship.

"Thank you Alice," she said, and turned quickly over on her side, drawing up the covers.

Until about noon I managed to keep the children occupied while Arden slept. Then she got up, looking startlingly fresh and energetic. Together we cleared the kitchen of rubble, cleaned and mopped, stored water in plastic jugs. Then we started on the living room, the next worst area, while the children played outside on the grass. In the sunshine they did not look like disaster victims but like inheritors of the earth.

When the telephone rang it startled me out of a world that already felt natural and customary. Chowder bleated at me through a bad connection. He was frantic with worry. Malthus was with him. They would come immediately but there were no flights available until next morning. They were relieved we were together.

Malthus wanted to know if his house was in any real danger. Arden shook her head no at me, smiled a slanted smile, and stirred the spaghetti sauce while Hillary crumpled basil leaves and dropped them in with great intention. Tomorrow at 3:40 P.M. they would arrive and take the limousine from the airport. We were to stay put until they got there.

"Me too," I said in that old code language designed to express feeling without acknowledging it. When I hung up I felt as if I had been visited by a flying saucer in some remote and desolate field, that no one would believe what I had seen and experienced. Then I felt a warm hand on my shoulder and looked up into Arden's shining eyes.

I felt swept and taken, as by a wave I had not thought to survive. I cried for just a minute, the first time in years, sitting on the kitchen chair with Hillary crowding her little face next to mine, smelling of basil. Was I sad, she asked? Had I hurt myself? Arden knelt and held us both, and I felt supported in what I was not understanding. There was a strong pressure on my back, against which I might lean without losing my self-respect, just as when Arden had arrived that morning she did not conceal from me her fear, but let me lead her off to rest and to restore herself.

This movement back and forth of need and support was as patterned as a dance yet as simple as two women cleaning a kitchen together, knowing how, from the endless kitchens they had cleaned alone.

Kip came in just then, looking earnest, wanting to know how to get water out of the spaghetti. We moved back toward the world of colanders and silverware on tables, relieved.

Everybody had a task in the kitchen except the baby. We sailed about like circus tumblers, evading one another as we looped from refrigerator to sink, stove to counter—Arthur after the parmesan cheese, Arden searching out garlic, Jamie slicing cautiously through celery, Hillary tearing leaves of lettuce, Max creasing napkins lengthwise, while Ellen crawled between our legs.

We sat at the large glass table that Chowder and I so seldom used because it dwarfed us. Now the table was full, in play. Arden and I tied dish towels about the necks of Max and Ellen, then sat down to our feast. There was warm champagne in everybody's glass. Arden lifted hers, catching a glint of candlelight.

"Love and friendship, everybody." And she smiled that wonderful smile.

After dinner I played the piano, then began rounds of baths, dishwashing, and finally bedding down. I was exhausted by the time the last child was asleep.

Out on the deck I leaned against the rail, feeling the cool, light breeze playing against my cheek. The sliding door opened and closed. I could just see Arden's outline against the moon as she came toward me.

"Tired?" she asked gently.

"A little," I conceded.

She laughed. "More than a little." She sank down in the chair at my side and filled two orange juice glasses with champagne. "This time it's properly iced."

When she handed up my glass, we touched momentarily, and I had that sense again of meaning beyond the usual, of casual acts taking on significance. How could I know this feeling as romance, when long ago I had consigned romance to the world of dreams?

I stretched and drank my champagne. We talked quietly, until the wind grew and chilled us. I suggested a fire in the music room.

If I say we built that fire together, some of you will understand and others will not.

A friend of mine once said, Whoever needs to build the fire will build the fire. There is wisdom in that, I know. But until this night with Arden I had always found myself with someone who needed to build the fire. Unless I was alone. Why else should I find solitude so welcome a guest?

But I felt in that room no one's need, beyond the simple desire to have a fire and to lie quietly before it on a few pillows. How long we lay there I can't say. When the fire burned low one of us would put a log on. When a glass emptied, someone opened a new bottle.

We did not touch. There was some care taken about that. Something studied where nothing else was.

I felt my own longing so palpable it was like a third person in the room. A longing with no ego to it. Refined yet growing more urgent. Finally asking something of me.

But where in my long history of lesson taking had I been taught to make a first move?

I do not mean the simple execution of the move but the sense of fitness and even right that justifies the move.

But it was impossible. At last I rose to go, hesitating only to give the fire one more stir. Behind me I was aware of Arden getting to her feet. She walked with me to the door, leaned against the jamb with the fire-light playing over her face, saying one more thing. And then one more.

Had the goddess given up on our own pitiful attempts? Suddenly there was a roar, a jolt, and a violent trembling that sent us grasping at last for one another's arms, where we held each other, caressed, murmured until the earth shuddered back to her slumbers. And still we held each other, touching tenderly, unbelievingly.

19

BEEF WELLINGTON

With the death of my aunt, my Indian self lay quietly down on her ancestor's funeral pyre, while my Avon lady aspect went efficiently about her business. In three months she had me secured in a Scorpio marriage, in four settled in a San Fernando Valley housing development, in five pregnant, in six incapable of writing a line of poetry.

Malthus took credit for the departure of the muse. Being a wife and mother diverted my creativity to socially useful paths, he believed. I had narrowly missed disaster in a brush with madness and death, handmaidens of poetry. Now I was free to fulfill myself.

Up to this point I knew very little about men, especially on a live-in basis. My father had died when I was six, and my mother contented herself with teaching school, caring for me and my older sisters, and reading cheap novels into the night. Of course Maurio, Michael, and Ramón were my friends, but I was never responsible for their laundry.

Once you agree to make yourself responsible for a man's laundry you sensitize yourself to his defects. You begin to notice his tendency to pee on the toilet seat. You begin to wish he preferred Kleenex to handkerchiefs. And finally you fail to understand why he interprets your growing inability to compose poetry as a sign of your freedom.

I am raising my children to do their own laundry. Otherwise friendship is not possible.

Malthus sometimes would ask me in perplexity if I had a theory of child rearing. I told him no.

Anyway, for twelve long years I persisted in this Scorpio marriage, quietly training my children to do their own laundry and to keep promises and to appreciate themselves. For twelve long years I kept on not writing poetry. For twelve long years the Avon lady had her way with me.

Then I went to a party with Malthus, another—apparently—in that endless chain of social events which were really business transactions in drag. This one I particularly dreaded because it was given by Malthus's new supervisor, a man who according to Malthus had nothing to recommend him but a Harvard accent. We almost didn't go at all because Arthur came down with what looked like chicken pox but later proved to be a rash he sometimes gets when he eats strawberries. So we went. Late.

Everybody was crowded into the living room, talking in polite but too loud tones, while somebody played the piano. Before I saw her I felt sorry for whoever was trying to play the piano in the din of the marketplace. When I saw her I quit.

Seated at the piano was simple power. Creative power. Music came out of her private solitude and searched the room—like a butterfly in a walled garden—for an answer. I didn't think anybody knew the answer to what she asked but me. I could hardly breathe. Listening to her like that.

And afterward there was no way of course to tell her. I could only gape, mumble, and shake her hand too hard and too long.

Hardly the lurid beginning you had hoped for. Right? You wanted a scene of seduction and satisfaction of your puerile curiosity about what women do in bed together. And I have left you with a picture of a pregnant woman over thirty gazing lyrically at a graying woman over forty, playing Cole Porter. People turn to pornography when they can't any longer see the magic in reality.

And though I had no interest in pornography, I was nearly as out of touch with magic as you, ravaged as we all are by acquisition, politics, and sophisticated self-doubt. We are all sitting, stunned, waiting for the Avon lady to ring.

I can't say I roused myself right away. But almost as if Aunt Vi were whispering in my ear, I began to yearn for travel, for poetry, for chance, for style, for friendship, for a Harley Davidson 350. I knew that I was in love with Alice Wicks in a steadfast, excited way, and was going to keep on, and that that fine feeling was making me shine again and hum. Poems began to spin off from me like rabbits from the highway.

Of course none of this was to Malthus's liking. Not that I mentioned either Alice Wicks or the Harley Davidson 350. Mostly it was the poetry and then finally it was my decision to return to school at thirty-three and work on a graduate degree in creative writing.

"But you're the mother of six!" he exclaimed in that pale, tight-lipped way.

Whenever I planned anything that violated Malthus's sensibility or threatened his comfort he would say, "But you're the mother of six!" as if like Moll Flanders I had lost count of my children in my lust for self-indulgence.

For twelve long years Malthus's tactic had worked, until one day— some time after I had heard Alice Wicks play "They're Writing Songs of Love But Not for Me"—I began to wonder why a mother of six should be required to give up more than other people. Perhaps she ought to be asked to give up less.

That same afternoon I applied for admission to graduate school and charged at Joseph Magnin's a midnight-blue leather jacket with lots of zippers, in anticipation of my new motorcycle.

So there were some plans in the works but none of them involved Alice and me or what might be done in the way of deepening or acknowledging a relationship.

I have a very organic approach to love. Hurrying Alice into feeling something for me, I thought, would be rather like shouting at a violet, "Well, bloom why don't you?" For better than a year I patiently tended my own garden. Until last February when the earth tilted herself and slid Alice and me together, lit a fire in the fireplace, and filled our glasses with champagne.

You are wondering what all this has to do with beef Wellington. I am coming to that. Because as you may have guessed by now, this beef Wellington is not merely a tenderloin of beef, wrapped in mushrooms and foie gras, and finally done up in a pastry puff. No. This is a symbolic beef Wellington.

Of course, the beef Wellington was these actual things—beef, mush-rooms, foie gras, pastry—but it came to represent, in the course of events, far more than the sum of its parts.

Now I did not want to serve beef Wellington at Malthus's dinner party in the first place. Partly because it takes three days to make, partly because these dinner parties were not celebrations but way stations for Malthus's tedious journey toward what he called success, and partly because of an objection I have toward French cooking.

Not all French cooking. Just the kind that aims to make a dish defy nature. For example, one recipe has you remove every bone from a duck's body, then stuff the duck meat back into the skin in such a way that until you bite into it you think every support is intact. Of course defying nature costs extra. These effects are not got up on the spur of the moment. They take three days, minimum.

And Malthus *would* have beef Wellington.

Well there were essentially two problems, one was in the dough and one was in my life. It was clear from Julia Child's recipe that this dough would have to be wrestled into obedience. I had encountered the same problem in her quiche recipe, where she had you spend two days preparing a light dough, then advised you how to conquer its natural tendency to rise. She said to sprinkle beans into the unbaked shell to keep it flat during baking. Lacking beans I tried Little Friskies and the kitchen smelled for three days.

Now she was telling me to restrain the beef Wellington dough with pieces of a meat grinder that weighed five pounds. I did not have a meat grinder.

Also there were other jolly warnings that intimated I might discover the foie gras had a tendency to fall off the tenderloin, that the slices of meat might stick together at serving time, and that the dough might very well be soggy.

But the warning that caused me most dis-ease sounded more psychological than culinary. "An important dish like this should be surrounded with few distractions," she cautioned. What Julia Child did not know was that in the case of my beef Wellington, distractions were as inevitable as foie gras. Because Alice Wicks would be there. And Chowder. For the first time since that memorable aftershock last February the entire rectangle would be assembled. It was not so much that I feared detection as I feared the outrage to Alice's and my feelings, having to conceal our rising spirits under five pounds of meat grinder.

I hung out a lot in the kitchen that night. It turned out two of the guests could not endure the sight of one another, precisely the kind of blunder in planning Malthus so abhorred. His solution was to keep the cocktails coming strong and frequent. Which only made the enemies less reserved in their animosity. Malthus kept knifing into the kitchen to ask if the beef Wellington was done. To probe the aspic. To run a thumb through the sliced almonds destined for the green beans.

When Malthus felt anger toward an inanimate object he generally transferred it to an animate one faster than you can say "beef Wellington." Consequently, the kind solicitude he felt toward the green beans almondine was—by the time his scrutinizing eye fell on me—no longer available. "Mix, can't you, for Christ's sake!" he whispered through gritted teeth.

I ripped off my hostess apron, picked up my drink, and stalked into the living room. And promptly melted. There was Alice, looking brave. Of course I wanted to go to her. That I couldn't made me angrier still. I really didn't understand why I must stand there awkwardly, instead of leaping onto the coffee table and yelling challenges at these intruders whose rights were presumed to exceed my own.

Instead I plunged my fingers absently into my martini glass after that olive, and murmured half articulately, "Oh, Julia!" When I looked up Malthus was staring at me, shaking his head in imperceptible admonishment. I looked over at Alice and saw that she saw, and that she had Malthus's number.

Malthus might miss signs of infidelity but he was radar sharp where conspiracy was concerned.

"Well, Alice," he said with insincere warmth, "you might play us a little something on the piano while we wait for the beef Wellington."

"There won't be time for that," I said in a menacing tone, wiping olive brine onto my hostess skirt.

Malthus shot me the look that means, And I'll see *you* in the kitchen. While he stayed behind momentarily, pouring oil on the waters, I stalked into the kitchen and yanked open the oven door on the beef Wellington. It looked like a football. Being French it was supposed to look like a football instead of a beef tenderloin.

When Malthus saw it his rage changed to gratitude and even reverence. Malthus has an inordinate appreciation, you see, for whatever truly defies its essence. That a beef tenderloin could be coaxed and cajoled into resembling a football filled him with delight and even optimism.

He must carve the football himself.

I really did try to caution him about Julia Child's concern over that pastry. Had she not in her concluding paragraph recommended slicing the top off the football before carving?

Feeling at home with this curious creation, Malthus believed himself competent to deal with its unique requirements. He sliced carefully crosswise, whereupon the entire pastry wrapping released its tenuous grasp on the roast and hit the floor.

"Malthus," I said, "I'm leaving you."

Well I know a symbol when I see one, but Malthus does not. He lives in the prison house of the literal. For a full three weeks he believed his wife of twelve long years left him because he ruined the beef Wellington.

I might have left well-enough alone, but somehow that he should fasten his guilt on a six-pound tenderloin seemed more than pathetic. When he feels at fault—which God knows is seldom enough—he looks more like William Holden than usual and can be difficult to resist. So I told him about Alice and me. I wish now I hadn't, of course. Because though that night he thanked me with tears in his eyes, the next morning on my way to school I saw in my rearview mirror the familiar set jaw and narrow gaze of Luther P. Grinwall, private investigator.

20

OVER MY DEAD BODY

Arden said she couldn't live her life as if it was a dance recital. So when the caseworker arrived, instead of wearing the respectable seersucker housedress Topaz had borrowed from a friend, Arden was lying under the school bus in her overalls.

Before that, she had been lying quietly in my arms in the still twenty minutes while the children slept and we kept watch over them and over each other. Arden and I had been living together a year but I never stopped feeling warmed by the easy way we moved from being the supported to the supporter and back again. That was the joy of it. Nobody got locked into limited, tedious, unchanging expressions of self. I held her now as if she floated in still water, my hand under her back.

"A penny," she said, in that low rich voice of hers, as she took my hand and kissed my palm.

"I was thinking about Winnifred Hooper coming today, and about Topaz's plans for putting your hair in pink curlers, and what really lies behind all that. The judgment, I mean, the power behind the judgment. It doesn't seem to come from anybody that really has to do with children."

"I think I know why that is, Dearest," she said, propping herself up on an elbow and smoothing the hair back from my brow.

"I think I know why, too, Dearest," said Hillary's voice just behind the door. "Can I come in now?"

The door flew open and the next instant Hillary jumped in bed with us, followed by the dog and Arthur, piping, "I know whyee, Dearest, yes I do."

We tickled and snuggled them until the laughter woke Max and Ellen, who also climbed into bed, sacking us with their pillows. Out in the hall we heard Topaz clear his throat discreetly.

"One more couldn't hurt," invited Arden from under the pillow.

Topaz came in with the seersucker housedress over his left arm and a bag of pink foam curlers in his right hand. "Is this the Brady Bunch?" he asked with a salacious grin.

"Listen Topaz," said Arden throwing back the covers and diving for the door. "No, Topaz, I won't have it. I said definitely no. Not the pink . . . " And they thundered down the hall and into Kip and Jamie, who had been heading up the hall with platters of French toast.

It was hard to believe in the enemy, in circumstances like these. But after we sorted ourselves at the picnic table that served as dinner table, after coffee and orange juice, and children dispatched to their Saturday projects, Topaz, Arden, and I were left with the question of Winnifred Hooper.

"Well," said Arden, rolling up her pajama sleeves and moving the saltshaker to the right of the pepper, "for my part, I am really and truly not going to put on those curlers and that housedress, not for Jesus Christ himself, and that's that."

Topaz took her face in his two hands and said, "Sometimes, Arden baby, you have got to play the man along to get what you want. Otherwise you wake up in the cage."

"Dear Topaz," Arden answered, kissing him lightly on the cheek, "I am not dealing with the man, as you put it. I'm dealing with Winnifred Hooper."

"Well, and who does Winnifred Hooper work for?" This time he looked at me, in a very straight and telling way that asked if I saw the danger Arden wasn't seeing.

It was no time to pretend I didn't understand. "Topaz is talking about risk, dear. And power."

"And who should know that better than I." Arden's voice was quiet, resonant, and unquestionable. That there was anger in it hardly touched our relationship. We were beyond ego skirmishes, moving now across mountains we had only read about.

How shall I describe Winnifred Hooper? Her eyes were the first thing one noticed. They were wistful and gray, on a narrow, almost gaunt face. But she was quite young, twenty-six or seven, and looked her youth, yet not in a conventional way. On the slender side, she was a good four or five inches taller than I, and held her head at a peculiar angle, as if as an adolescent she had worried she might be growing too tall. She wore a simple white blouse and a linen skirt with a dark, flowered pattern, canvas shoes with rope soles, and no makeup.

She was painfully shy. I invited her into the living room and brought coffee. I had some coward's impulse to whisk her straight out to Arden, but resisted. Not because I knew Arden was lying under the bus in her overalls, but because I knew Winnifred Hooper had business with me, quite as much as with Arden, and that she would know it. That was the feeling I had about her: that she knew very well what she was doing but that she seldom gave that impression.

Out of her straw bag she pulled a sheaf of forms, selected the appropriate one, and began penciling in one-word answers. How many bedrooms were there, how many baths, did we have a dishwasher, did the children ask questions about our relationship, had I finished college? Between questions she would apologize, keeping her gaze directed at the paper work. I led her through the house and out to Arden, who came rolling from under the bus on a grease monkey's cart, smiling and pleased, her natural self that I so extravagantly loved.

Arden showed her around the back yard, introducing her to the children as she went, saving Jamie and her science project for last. Jamie's class had been working on an energy unit, concentrating on sources of energy besides gas and oil. Jamie had said bunnies were a source of energy and Robert Wattle had said, "Oh shit," and everybody had laughed. After school Jamie had bloodied Robert Wattle's nose. Then she came home and began sketches that would have put Leonardo da Vinci's airplane designs to shame. Finally she had settled on a greenhouse that was to be warmed in winter by fans blowing through bunny ears.

We rounded the corner of the garage, where Jamie was nailing sheets of plastic over the skeleton of the four-by-four greenhouse. Arden stopped dead in her tracks at the sight of her eldest daughter in a blue voile dress, wielding a hammer. If Winnifred Hooper noticed either the dress or Arden, she didn't blench, but went straight up and introduced herself in that soft voice that went with her gray eyes, and asked Jamie about the fifth grade science project. Jamie glanced uneasily at her mother, then at me, and then began explicating her pastel rendering of a bunny's ear, a picture so strangely compelling it convinced you instantly that the crimson network was after all charged with such energy that nuclear power was soon to be a joke.

Just then Hillary, the seven-year-old, came up and said Kip wouldn't make lunch.

"That's not negotiable," said Arden, easing herself into the ordinary. "Kip always makes lunch on Saturday."

"Well he says he won't if he can't be Orlando when we play Shakespeare tonight."

"Copernicus!" shouted Arden in the direction of the kitchen window. "You know damn well what I think of blackmail."

"Mom, he can be Orlando. I'll be Rosalind."

Arden gave Jamie a long, hard look, and she burst into tears. Then Arden went down on her knees, holding her. I suggested Miss Hooper wait inside, and sent Hillary in with her.

"Are you pissed about the dress, Mom?"

"What's the dress code say in our family?"

"Comfortable and amusing."

"Clean, comfortable, and amusing," Arden gently corrected.

"Well who am I supposed to be amusing?" Jamie inquired, testing a loose front tooth.

"Yourself, duck," she said squeezing her daughter. "Yourself first and maybe others, if they are up to it and you like them enough."

"I guess I got scared."

"We're all scared, dear. Alice is scared, I'm scared, Topaz is scared, Earl is scared, Ben, Honey, Jim. People you've never even heard of are scared."

"Malthus is weird, Mom. I don't want to live with Malthus."

"Over my dead body," said Arden, scooping Jamie up in her arms and heading for the house.

Inside, Winnifred Hooper was leaning against the bookcase holding a sign that said "Forest of Arden," looking pale and overcome. Hillary had her by the hand and was shrieking at Topaz, "I am the second son of old Sir Rowland."

"Cut, cut," said Arden with a gesture nobody would mistake. "Take five."

Everybody scattered, except Topaz, who joined us at the door, where Winnifred Hooper was assembling her papers in her straw bag, murmuring, "I really must, I really must . . . "

"Have you met our sitter and friend, Topaz Wilson?"

"Yes, in a way," she said faintly, dropping her bag as she took Topaz's hand. "And now I really must . . . But I will see you again, you understand, twice this month, unannounced visits." And she was gone.

"Sweet Jesus," said Topaz, collapsing on the couch, "but we blew that one."

I really didn't know if we had or not, but neither of us had a chance to answer anyway. The door flew open and Ben Griffin, our feed man, rushed in, dropped a hundred-pound sack of rabbit food onto the living room rug, and said he never forgot a face. Then Kip leapt through the hall door with a mop on his head, exclaiming, "Do you not know I am a woman? When I think, I must speak. Sweet, say on."

"What is this ruckus about?" said Ben.

"Later Rosalind," said Arden, waving Kip back out of the room. "Now what were you . . . "

"I said I never do forget a face," said Ben, collecting his momentum, "like I told you. So I seen this lady come out of your house and I've got that there feed sack hoisted up onto my shoulder, but I kind of look over it and around it and I'm just about 99 percent sure what I'm talking about."

We all looked at him in amazement. Finally Topaz admitted he didn't understand.

"What I'm saying is this: that's Winnifred Hooper just been to your house."

"Well, of course it's Winnifred Hooper," laughed Arden.

"What I'm saying is that's Big Jim Muncey's Winnifred Hooper, that run away with the used car salesman from Chula Vista three years ago last May."

"Ah ha," said Topaz, significantly.

"You can forget that, Topaz," said Arden. "We are not power brokers here."

"We are not total assholes, either."

"Topaz," called Kip in a lilting voice, still with the mop on his head, "you know damn well what Mom thinks of blackmail."

"Thank you, fair Rosalind," said Arden, blowing Kip a kiss.

"I mean it," said Topaz. "Let's face it, we didn't stack up today as the Brady Bunch."

"You're being paranoid. I think we did very well."

Ben sat down in the chair next to the couch, motioning us to join him. Arden took my hand, kissed me softly, and the three of us sat down with Ben.

"Now I know none of this is my business," he began.

"Nonsense, Ben," said Arden, "you're one of the family."

"Thank you, Arden. Now as I see it we got to get Winnifred Hooper over to our side if we mean to keep them kids, and we do. My daddy always said to me, 'Ben, boy, it ain't what you know but who you know.' Now you see what I'm getting at? Big Jim don't hardly say two words without it's Winnifred this and Winnie that. What's the harm in doing both of them a favor and us at the same time?"

"Ben," called Kip from the hall, "you know how Mom feels about . . . "

"You bite your tongue, Rosalind. I guess I know your mom well enough."

"Yes, Ben, and you're perfectly right," Arden said emphatically. "It *is* who you know."

Ben's mouth fell wide open and Topaz bit his lip in amusement.

"It's like this," Arden continued, sketching a pattern with her finger on her outstretched palm, "you all remember Aunt Vi and Michael Raven. Well, you know Michael and have heard me tell about Aunt Vi. That summer in Mexico—oh, a dozen years ago—when Michael was following us, I thought of him as a spy, somebody from outside sent to stop us in our adventure. I wanted to jump him some moonless night and slit his throat. But Aunt Vi knew he belonged with us. She simply waited until he came to understand—by himself—that he was a member of our party. And Winnifred Hooper will do the same."

21

LIFE OF THE PARTY

Thirteen has got to be my lucky number. I was born April thirteenth, so was my mother, and so was my dear friend Arden. Can you beat this now? It is thirteen years since I have seen Arden Benbow. I know she is in trouble again because of these questions I keep getting from lawyers, detectives, and other snoops about her and Maurio and Vi, questions that set off my remembering like an explorer into the Arctic. I move around in my memories. I sleep my memories. Then the phone rings (June thirteenth, and that's the gospel). At first I think it is Vi and am startled and excited, thinking that if anybody can place such a call, it is Vi. But even when I get sensible with myself and recognize the voice as Arden's I do not calm down because I know something is about to happen again. And this time I am not letting that circus go piping out of the campground without old Ruby. Hell no.

Arden is inviting me. She says it is to be a loud and tender celebration of mother right, or some such, and that there is to be a wedding, and that Maurio and Michael will be there. I do not wait through the crackling and humming Mexican telephone system for any explanations about what is being celebrated or who is marrying who. All I ask is where and when, and I am packing my bags next minute.

I have this idea. Actually it's a dream. I want to go back to San Francisco to where I was the Girl on the Red Swing and I want to look up like a regular customer and see what it was they saw when I swung out. (I am not talking about sex.) Then I want to take the train down the coast to L.A. Ramón helps me plan it. The wedding will be August eighteenth and that leaves just enough time for my dream before the party begins.

Next morning Ramón drives me in to Guaymas. He is telling me not to worry about anything and flashing smiles sideways as he drives the truck down 15, but it strikes me suddenly that Ramón is older than he used to be, and for a minute I feel afraid for him. Then I remember he is a good twenty years younger than I am and laugh at thinking I will go on forever.

These are serious thoughts, but travel makes you have them, otherwise who would bother?

I look in the truck bed at my two suitcases. I really do not believe I will die. My tickets are in my purse. Ramón is searching for a parking place.

That day I only get as far as Mexico City. I check into the Reforma, where I stay whenever I come to town. In the bar I have three margaritas and strike up a conversation with two American businessmen. They are advising me how to invest my money and winking at two Mexican girls sitting across from us. Because of the girls, they are not paying attention to what they say, and I am not paying attention because investment bores me, though I know as much about it as I care to and have made as much money as I care about making.

Cute as they are, I feel restless to be off and alone somewhere. When you've been around as long as I have (seventy-one last April), these flirtations begin to seem off the point. So I go for a walk and have dinner back at the hotel. I am hungering for my friends but kind of enjoying coming at the party in an indirect way, lingering over the quiet so that when gaiety busts in he will seem more the rascal.

The next morning I catch a direct flight to San Francisco. First class. There is champagne and a movie about Art Carney and his cat. There is something mild and pretty about Art Carney and his cat, and about the champagne, as if I watch through fall colors and am not called upon to say this and that. We have fresh asparagus, and a fine layer of sliced almonds shines off the gentle slope of the chicken breast.

It is cold in San Francisco. On the pavement outside, held in a wedge of people needing cabs, I nudge my two suitcases forward. Wind whips at the coat I have remembered to bring. With three nuns I ride toward the St. Francis. "Jesus, it's cold," I say. They smile.

That night the nuns attend a banquet honoring the archbishop, and I go to North Beach. The cabby seems to think I have made a mistake, so I wink and tell him to keep the change.

Things are much the same. There is that same prowling energy that comes up out of the sidewalk like we are on a trolley line. Hucksters on the street, hookers, pimps, junkies, and Salvation Army captains. But nobody in military. Real military. Oh, they're there, alright, but cruising around in civvies, given away by their shaved heads and hungry looks. I had no more business with them, and I liked that freedom. I liked being alone and being Ruby in my cold city. Ruby on her way to a party.

At the Red Swing Bar I stop and look up. Nothing doing. It is Sid's Lounge now. The window I used to stand in before launching out is part of a Chinese restaurant. I can see bamboo in pots, and a table or two, shadows of people.

But I have come a long way and am not about to let loose of that dream yet. The thing about dreams is you can't order them up like ham and eggs. Sometimes you've got to hang back and let them come to you. So I fix myself just opposite my window, out of the way of the milling deadbeats, and prepare to let that dream seduce me.

Now you think I'm going to tell you I saw myself poised in that window wearing my red sequined G-string with the feathers fore and aft and that I saw myself swing out over gaping sailors and heard their roar of appreciation. You've seen too many movies.

No, my memory is old and honest and doesn't go in for costuming and stage props anymore. Let's just say I found what I came for, saw what I came to see.

Afterwards I am hungry but don't want to risk the Chinese restaurant. Because of the dream, you know. As I turn to go, I hear someone call my name. I look back, and in my window next to the potted bamboo stands Michael Raven, all grown up and cute as ever. His face is lit like a Chinese lantern and he is gesturing to me to wait, and to whoever he's with to hurry up, and a minute later he runs out the front door, followed by a tall blond. Well he hugs me and kisses me and gambols and frolics around so that I see he has finally figured out about delight and so forth. He is introducing me to his girl, when out pops Maurio, dressed fit to kill but of course still only five foot four in his stocking feet, and he is with a Japanese gentleman not much taller but with considerably more hair. Another round of hugs and kisses follows, topped off with a magic trick or two.

"So this is Ruby. So this is Ruby," chants the tall blond, shaking her head like she has been introduced to a queen.

Finally we all calm down a little, but not much, and I find out the tall blond is Allison Honey and that the Japanese gentleman is Royce Woo and that he is an architect. They have been celebrating Honey's promotion to head chef at Raven and Carbonara, Caterers. They have also been planning a little trip.

Next thing I know I've got Michael on my right and Maurio on my left, with Royce and Honey behind, and we are marching straight in to Sid's Lounge. But I am not feeling protective of my dream any longer. The dream feels sturdy and at ease.

We sit down at a large booth in the corner. There is a fishnet on the wall behind, with dead things caught in it but arranged to look alive and on the move. A candle set into a cork float flickers on the table. Everybody is looking at us. Joy has that effect, you know. People warm themselves by it. I look back at them so they will feel welcome, and Michael hugs me again. Maurio waves his hand over the candle telling it to go out, but it does not go out, and Honey laughs and shakes her long bright hair. Royce is bent over his cocktail napkin, working with a thick pencil.

Across the room I spot two of my nuns from St. Francis. I feel like I want to bless them. I have the waitress take them a couple of mai tai cocktails, compliments of the archbishop. They look up at me and smile. *Sister* is such a word, I think.

Royce hands me his napkin and tells me he has done my portrait. It is a sketch of a tall, spreading house with porches and balconies off every door and window.

I thank him. At seventy you don't have to pretend not to understand when someone comes that close. You can just say thank you and order everybody another round which is exactly what I did.

Then Honey says she wants some fortune cookies. Royce goes upstairs and brings down a plateful from the Chinese restaurant. Thoughtfully she passes around the plate as if she knows for sure each of us will get just the right cookie. I open mine up. It says, "Let me read with open eyes the book my days are writing." Honey smiles at me but she doesn't ask, like people usually do, what it says. She just smiles.

On account of my fortune I feel like I want some air and that very soon I will want to stretch out on hotel sheets and let the day enter into my sleeping mind. I feel simple.

All this I tell my friends, because when you are seventy you may as well say what you need and be done with it. Inside half an hour I get my wish, but not before I have agreed to drive down with them to the party tomorrow.

That night I am like a body in a canoe being carried from inlet to inlet until at last I nudge ashore and sit upright in my canoe, listening, as if someone has spoken. Daytime sounds of delivery trucks and rumbling cable come through gauzy curtains. I order breakfast. I sit in the window on the twenty-sixth floor of the St. Francis Hotel, waiting. My nuns gather below on the sidewalk, then funnel themselves into a cab, like ink into a bottle, and are gone.

The eggs arrive cold, making me miss Ramón and mangoes from my garden. I sit in the window sipping coffee, feeling the breeze from the bay whiffle my head and brush my cheeks. Adventure sometimes starts slow, like a knowing and tender lover.

By eight I have bathed, packed my few belongings, and am waiting on the sidewalk for my friends. At last they pull up in a canary yellow van that says Raven and Carbonara, Caterers on the side. Michael and Maurio pop out either door, and help me into the back, where Honey is sitting next to a towering wedding cake.

She jumps up and hugs me, steering me past the cake toward a seat. We are off. The sun shines and glints off the bay. I try to get Honey to join me by the window, but she is afraid to leave the cake.

And to tell the truth, there is something about that cake. Instead of tapering up in layers, each one is the same size with a space in between, making you feel like you could just walk into that cake and spend a week or two without getting bored.

"Where's Royce?" I asked, suddenly making the connection.

Honey laughed and motioned me over to the cake. At the very bottom, in a thin squiggle of rose-colored frosting, the cake was signed, "Honey & Woo."

"He couldn't make it but he said he would be there anyway, through his art." She laughed again in that way she had of reminding you her name was Honey.

For three hundred miles we told stories, napped a little, drank chablis, and ate crackers with paté. After a while that cake felt like a tree we were lying under.

I wanted to stop, stretch my toes in the Pacific, but we were running late and the party kept muscling into my mind and making me feel glad to hurry. Something felt right about making the last leg of my journey in a rush. Finally we left the Pacific and wound eastward over coastal hills and into the valley where Arden lived.

In the front yard was nobody. I was afraid they had started without us. Maurio and Michael ran into the house to dress, but I was ready and so was Honey. We just stopped in the hall for a look-see in the mirror and out into the back yard where ninety-nine people were milling around and asking each other what time it was. Over this questioning rose a handsome black face. Then I lost sight of him, and then he touched me on the elbow, and bent down toward me looking kindly and full of mischief at the same time.

"Ruby Red from San Francisco, meet Topaz Black from Pacoima." He whipped a sapphire blue top hat from his head and bowed low. Then he caught Honey up and waltzed her around on the grass until they banged into an old lady with henna red hair, dressed in her robe and slippers.

"I'm a guest of Violet Groot," the old lady said crossly.

Topaz bowed low and said Mrs. Groot couldn't make it, but that whoever she was she was most welcome.

Just then Maurio came up wearing a black tuxedo with sequins on the lapel. "Mrs. Wall," he said, pulling a gold coin from her ear and kissing her on her fuzzy old cheek.

"Maurio! Maurio Carbonara!"

Arm in arm they walked off toward the rows of folding chairs, and when she turned I saw embroidered across the back of her robe, "Thousand Oaks Rest Home."

It's starting, I think. It's starting.

Just then Topaz Black jumps up on the little stage in front of the lines of folding chairs. "Ladies and Gentlemen. Ladies and Gentlemen. The ceremonial part of our celebration is about to begin. Please take your seats."

There is more humming and confusion, but finally everybody is more or less settled, except for a big shaggy dog running around wearing a sign saying, "Champion Bloodlines. Ask for Big Jim Muncey."

Then Topaz Black raises his arms for quiet and gets it. He must be six foot four in his stocking feet. "Ladies and Gentlemen. Welcome and welcome again to this loud, tender party. We gather together this day to celebrate not one but three beautiful events. The first—as many of you know—is a double wedding." He gestures toward the window of the house and everybody breaks into applause and cheers. I see Arden, dressed up like an Indian, standing close to the glass and somebody in a white tuxedo just behind, and more, but I can't make out what.

Then Topaz Black proceeds. "The second," he says, trying to calm people down with his height and his steady gaze, "the second is the thirteenth anniversary of Violet Groot's death."

"Rest in peace," says the red-haired old lady, struggling to her feet.

"Not likely," says a gentle, amused voice just behind her. And everybody kind of smiles around at each other.

"And last but by no means least," continues Topaz Black, after a respectful silence, "is the happy conclusion of the custody trial." Here there is mad cheering, and six kids get up from the front row, face the audience, shooting embarrassed kid-smiles, and sit back down.

Topaz Black raises his hands again for quiet. "Let me introduce to you now the person who will perform the marriage ceremony. She is also the person whose expert testimony decided the custody issue. I give you Winnifred Hooper, M.S.W., former investigator for the Child Welfare Division, County of Los Angeles."

There is thunderous applause and a slim, pale woman of about twenty-six or so gets up, looking like she will just die of shyness. She clears her throat a couple of times and nods in the direction of the house.

The screen door bangs open and Arden steps out in her buckskins on the arm of Michael Raven, in a snow white tuxedo. From where the kids sit, the wavering sound of a penny whistle starts up. The door bangs shut behind them as they walk toward Winnifred Hooper, M.S.W. Door bangs open again and out comes a short lady wearing a long black dress, her hand on the arm of Maurio. They make for the front too. Seems like they must be the bridesmaid and best man, but by the time they get there Honey has stood up too and a man I don't know, with a cutaway and a beer belly. Then Arden and Michael and the short lady in the long black dress and Maurio all kneel down before Winnifred Hooper, M.S.W., who clears her throat one more time and strikes out at last.

"By the authority invested in me as a notary public . . ."

Here she is interrupted by a thick-chested man at the back of the audience saying, "Winnifred, is that you? Is that you dear?" He is wearing bib overalls and a flannel shirt, is half standing up, with people all around trying to get him to sit down and hush.

She looks at him like she can't believe her eyes and gets even paler, if that's possible. Then, remembering where she is, she starts clearing her throat, striking out again in that soft voice so she can get the whole thing over and done.

It's harder for her than it would be for most, but she goes on and lots goes by I can't quite catch, with every now and then the man's voice breaking through and saying, "Winnifred, is that you dear?"

Finally it sounds like she is nearing the finish line, when out pops this rabbit. Jesus but it's a big one. Comes out of the bushes and hunches there listening, wiggling his nose and thinking over whatever Winnifred Hooper has to say. Of course it's just a matter of time till that shaggy dog that's with the big-chested man catches the scent. Finally it does, but one of the kids grabs for its collar. The sign saying "Champion Blood-lines" goes flying, dog and kid go crashing into the next row of seats, rabbit disappears, and the back-row voice asks again, "Winnifred, is that you dear?"

Whether it is or not, she has decided to settle one thing at a time. "As the immortal George Eliot wrote," she says, glancing at her Benrus, marriage is still a great beginning. It is the beginning of the home epic . . . "

But Winnifred has lost her train of thought and no wonder. The kid with the penny whistle, thinking she has finished, begins to pipe the "Triumphal March," while the red-haired old lady swipes at him with her purse. "Beginning of the home epic . . . which makes the advancing years a climax, and age the harvest of sweet memories in common!"

Winnifred, looking relieved, now says to the two couples, "Is each of you devoted to the joy and freedom of the other?" Then the four say, "I am."

Winnifred draws herself up, clears her throat one last time, and says, "Welcome to the quest of the home epic. You may kiss." Then she sinks down in a folding chair, the kid strikes up the "Triumphal March" again, while Michael turns and kisses Maurio, and Arden turns and kisses the short lady in the long black dress.

Well I am so struck with admiration I hardly notice when the man in the flannel shirt goes running toward Winnifred, and the dog after him, dragging on his cuff. Finally he catches her up in his arms so that she almost disappears.

I do wish for Ramón. He loves a commotion.

Afterwards everybody went into the house for refreshments. At first I could hardly see, moving from afternoon sun into the shade of Arden's house. The best man put a glass of champagne into my hand, saying he was Earl, friend of the family. Behind me I heard a sliding around, like sandpaper rubbed together. It was Topaz Black doing a tap dance. He looked just like Fred Astaire, only taller of course.

Then I saw Honey and Royce's cake on the table, with Honey standing just behind and Arden next to her, admiring, while Maurio cut the first slice. He handed it to the henna-headed old lady, who had to bang the shaggy dog across the chops to keep it. Then Arden saw me and threw out her arms, with that warm call, "Ruby." It felt good to hold her. She was not a girl anymore, but she had that energy, the same that came out of Vi and shimmered over our lives thirteen years ago.

Earl filled our glasses again, and then Arden guided me about the room, introducing me to as many of her kids as would hold still long enough, and then to her lover, Alice Wicks, the short lady in the long black dress, who had dear warm eyes and when she sat down to the piano played "Ruby."

I can't even remember everybody I met. There was a Maude Calisher, who was Aunt Vi's cell mate, if I heard right, and who kept following me around trying to tell me the story of Chicken Little and the Eighteen-Hour Girdle, or some such. And there was a big fellow named Ben Griffin, a friend of the man in the flannel shirt, who it turned out used to be engaged to Winnifred Hooper but hadn't seen her in years—Ben said—until just now and so it wasn't any wonder the way he kept calling her name while she was trying to get through the ceremony.

Finally I sat down with Winnifred Hooper and Big Jim (the man in the flannel shirt) and the shaggy dog to tell her how I liked what she said about the home epic. She said she didn't make it up, but thanked me anyway. I asked her what was this business of the custody trial, and she said that when she first came out to see them she thought it wasn't much of a family but the more she came they kind of grew on her until one night a rabbit got loose and they were all chasing it around the trees and she fell into Kip and Kip fell into Jamie and Jamie fell into Earl and so forth and that when she got up she found she was in love with the whole family, regardless of Mrs. Renninger's professional opinion.

Mrs. Renninger's professional opinion ran along the lines of fault, and nobody saw things that way anymore, at least she thought they didn't, and that anyway the more she tried to figure where the fault lay the less she understood what the question was.

Winnifred took a deep sip of her champagne and brushed a damp strand out of her eyes, looking surprised at her long speech. "Well, it makes me mad," she said.

"That's right, my darling," said Big Jim, squeezing her shoulders too hard. "Arden Benbow is one fine woman, and anybody says different better not say so around Big Jim Muncey." He held up his glass toward Arden Benbow, standing by the cake, hand in hand with Alice. "Long and happy life," he boomed.

Arden raised hers to him, and in the voice of her Aunt Vi answered, "Love and friendship, everybody!"

I always was a sucker for a happy ending.

A few of the publications of
THE NAIAD PRESS, INC.
P.O. Box 10543 • Tallahassee, Florida 32302
Phone (904) 539-5965
Toll-Free Order Number: 1-800-533-1973
Mail orders welcome. Please include 15% postage.

FOREVER by Evelyn Kennedy. 224 pp. Passionate romance — love overcoming all obstacles.   ISBN 1-56280-094-9 $10.95

WHISPERS by Kris Bruyer. 176 pp. Romantic ghost story
ISBN 1-56280-082-5   10.95

NIGHT SONGS by Penny Mickelbury. 224 pp. A Gianna Maglione Mystery. Second in a series.   ISBN 1-56280-097-3   10.95

GETTING TO THE POINT by Teresa Stores. 256 pp. Classic southern Lesbian novel.   ISBN 1-56280-100-7   10.95

PAINTED MOON by Karin Kallmaker. 224 pp. Delicious Kallmaker romance.   ISBN 1-56280-075-2   9.95

THE MYSTERIOUS NAIAD edited by Katherine V. Forrest & Barbara Grier. 320 pp. Love stories by Naiad Press authors.
ISBN 1-56280-074-4   14.95

DAUGHTERS OF A CORAL DAWN by Katherine V. Forrest. 240 pp. Tenth Anniversary Edition.   ISBN 1-56280-104-X   10.95

BODY GUARD by Claire McNab. 208 pp. A Carol Ashton Mystery. 6th in a series.   ISBN 1-56280-073-6   9.95

CACTUS LOVE by Lee Lynch. 192 pp. Stories by the beloved storyteller.   ISBN 1-56280-071-X   9.95

SECOND GUESS by Rose Beecham. 216 pp. An Amanda Valentine Mystery. 2nd in a series.   ISBN 1-56280-069-8   9.95

THE SURE THING by Melissa Hartman. 208 pp. L.A. earthquake romance.   ISBN 1-56280-078-7   9.95

A RAGE OF MAIDENS by Lauren Wright Douglas. 240 pp. A Caitlin Reece Mystery. 6th in a series.   ISBN 1-56280-068-X   9.95

TRIPLE EXPOSURE by Jackie Calhoun. 224 pp. Romantic drama involving many characters.   ISBN 1-56280-067-1   9.95

UP, UP AND AWAY by Catherine Ennis. 192 pp. Delightful romance.   ISBN 1-56280-065-5   9.95

PERSONAL ADS by Robbi Sommers. 176 pp. Sizzling short stories.   ISBN 1-56280-059-0   9.95

FLASHPOINT by Katherine V. Forrest. 256 pp. Lesbian
blockbuster! ISBN 1-56280-043-4 22.95

CROSSWORDS by Penny Sumner. 256 pp. 2nd Victoria Cross
Mystery. ISBN 1-56280-064-7 9.95

SWEET CHERRY WINE by Carol Schmidt. 224 pp. A novel of
suspense. ISBN 1-56280-063-9 9.95

CERTAIN SMILES by Dorothy Tell. 160 pp. Erotic short stories.
ISBN 1-56280-066-3 9.95

EDITED OUT by Lisa Haddock. 224 pp. 1st Carmen Ramirez
Mystery. ISBN 1-56280-077-9 9.95

WEDNESDAY NIGHTS by Camarin Grae. 288 pp. Sexy
adventure. ISBN 1-56280-060-4 10.95

SMOKEY O by Celia Cohen. 176 pp. Relationships on the
playing field. ISBN 1-56280-057-4 9.95

KATHLEEN O'DONALD by Penny Hayes. 256 pp. Rose and
Kathleen find each other and employment in 1909 NYC.
ISBN 1-56280-070-1 9.95

STAYING HOME by Elisabeth Nonas. 256 pp. Molly and Alix
want a baby . . . or do they? ISBN 1-56280-076-0 10.95

TRUE LOVE by Jennifer Fulton. 240 pp. Six lesbians searching
for love in all the "right" places. ISBN 1-56280-035-3 9.95

GARDENIAS WHERE THERE ARE NONE by Molleen Zanger.
176 pp. Why is Melanie inextricably drawn to the old house?
ISBN 1-56280-056-6 9.95

KEEPING SECRETS by Penny Mickelbury. 208 pp. A Gianna
Maglione Mystery. First in a series. ISBN 1-56280-052-3 9.95

THE ROMANTIC NAIAD edited by Katherine V. Forrest &
Barbara Grier. 336 pp. Love stories by Naiad Press authors.
ISBN 1-56280-054-X 14.95

UNDER MY SKIN by Jaye Maiman. 336 pp. A Robin Miller
mystery. 3rd in a series. ISBN 1-56280-049-3. 10.95

STAY TOONED by Rhonda Dicksion. 144 pp. Cartoons — 1st
collection since *Lesbian Survival Manual.* ISBN 1-56280-045-0 9.95

CAR POOL by Karin Kallmaker. 272pp. Lesbians on wheels
and then some! ISBN 1-56280-048-5 9.95

NOT TELLING MOTHER: STORIES FROM A LIFE by Diane
Salvatore. 176 pp. Her 3rd novel. ISBN 1-56280-044-2 9.95

GOBLIN MARKET by Lauren Wright Douglas. 240pp. A Caitlin
Reece Mystery. 5th in a series. ISBN 1-56280-047-7 10.95

LONG GOODBYES by Nikki Baker. 256 pp. A Virginia Kelly
mystery. 3rd in a series. ISBN 1-56280-042-6 9.95

FRIENDS AND LOVERS by Jackie Calhoun. 224 pp. Mid-western
Lesbian lives and loves.   ISBN 1-56280-041-8   10.95

THE CAT CAME BACK by Hilary Mullins. 208 pp. Highly
praised Lesbian novel.   ISBN 1-56280-040-X   9.95

BEHIND CLOSED DOORS by Robbi Sommers. 192 pp. Hot,
erotic short stories.   ISBN 1-56280-039-6   9.95

CLAIRE OF THE MOON by Nicole Conn. 192 pp. See the
movie — read the book!   ISBN 1-56280-038-8   10.95

SILENT HEART by Claire McNab. 192 pp. Exotic Lesbian
romance.   ISBN 1-56280-036-1   10.95

HAPPY ENDINGS by Kate Brandt. 272 pp. Intimate conversations
with Lesbian authors.   ISBN 1-56280-050-7   10.95

THE SPY IN QUESTION by Amanda Kyle Williams. 256 pp.
4th Madison McGuire.   ISBN 1-56280-037-X   9.95

SAVING GRACE by Jennifer Fulton. 240 pp. Adventure and
romantic entanglement.   ISBN 1-56280-051-5   9.95

THE YEAR SEVEN by Molleen Zanger. 208 pp. Women surviving
in a new world.   ISBN 1-56280-034-5   9.95

CURIOUS WINE by Katherine V. Forrest. 176 pp. Tenth Anniver-
sary Edition. The most popular contemporary Lesbian love story.
                                            ISBN 1-56280-053-1   10.95
        Audio Book (2 cassettes)   ISBN 1-56280-105-8   16.95

CHAUTAUQUA by Catherine Ennis. 192 pp. Exciting, romantic
adventure.   ISBN 1-56280-032-9   9.95

A PROPER BURIAL by Pat Welch. 192 pp. A Helen Black
mystery. 3rd in a series.   ISBN 1-56280-033-7   9.95

SILVERLAKE HEAT: A Novel of Suspense by Carol Schmidt.
240 pp. Rhonda is as hot as Laney's dreams. ISBN 1-56280-031-0   9.95

LOVE, ZENA BETH by Diane Salvatore. 224 pp. The most talked
about lesbian novel of the nineties!   ISBN 1-56280-030-2   10.95

A DOORYARD FULL OF FLOWERS by Isabel Miller. 160 pp.
Stories incl. 2 sequels to *Patience and Sarah*.   ISBN 1-56280-029-9   9.95

MURDER BY TRADITION by Katherine V. Forrest. 288 pp. A
Kate Delafield Mystery. 4th in a series.   ISBN 1-56280-002-7   9.95

THE EROTIC NAIAD edited by Katherine V. Forrest & Barbara
Grier. 224 pp. Love stories by Naiad Press authors.
                                            ISBN 1-56280-026-4   13.95

DEAD CERTAIN by Claire McNab. 224 pp. A Carol Ashton
mystery. 5th in a series.   ISBN 1-56280-027-2   9.95

CRAZY FOR LOVING by Jaye Maiman. 320 pp. A Robin Miller
mystery. 2nd in a series.   ISBN 1-56280-025-6   9.95

STONEHURST by Barbara Johnson. 176 pp. Passionate regency
romance.   ISBN 1-56280-024-8   9.95

INTRODUCING AMANDA VALENTINE by Rose Beecham.
256 pp. An Amanda Valentine Mystery. First in a series.
                                                 ISBN 1-56280-021-3   9.95

UNCERTAIN COMPANIONS by Robbi Sommers. 204 pp.
Steamy, erotic novel.   ISBN 1-56280-017-5   9.95

A TIGER'S HEART by Lauren W. Douglas. 240 pp. A Caitlin
Reece mystery. 4th in a series.   ISBN 1-56280-018-3   9.95

PAPERBACK ROMANCE by Karin Kallmaker. 256 pp. A
delicious romance.   ISBN 1-56280-019-1   9.95

MORTON RIVER VALLEY by Lee Lynch. 304 pp. Lee Lynch
at her best!   ISBN 1-56280-016-7   9.95

THE LAVENDER HOUSE MURDER by Nikki Baker. 224 pp.
A Virginia Kelly Mystery. 2nd in a series.   ISBN 1-56280-012-4   9.95

PASSION BAY by Jennifer Fulton. 224 pp. Passionate romance,
virgin beaches, tropical skies.   ISBN 1-56280-028-0   10.95

STICKS AND STONES by Jackie Calhoun. 208 pp. Contemporary
lesbian lives and loves.   ISBN 1-56280-020-5   9.95
Audio Book (2 cassettes)   ISBN 1-56280-106-6   16.95

DELIA IRONFOOT by Jeane Harris. 192 pp. Adventure for Delia
and Beth in the Utah mountains.   ISBN 1-56280-014-0   9.95

UNDER THE SOUTHERN CROSS by Claire McNab. 192 pp.
Romantic nights Down Under.   ISBN 1-56280-011-6   9.95

GRASSY FLATS by Penny Hayes. 256 pp. Lesbian romance in
the '30s.   ISBN 1-56280-010-8   9.95

A SINGULAR SPY by Amanda K. Williams. 192 pp. 3rd
Madison McGuire.   ISBN 1-56280-008-6   8.95

THE END OF APRIL by Penny Sumner. 240 pp. A Victoria
Cross mystery. First in a series.   ISBN 1-56280-007-8   8.95

HOUSTON TOWN by Deborah Powell. 208 pp. A Hollis
Carpenter mystery.   ISBN 1-56280-006-X   8.95

KISS AND TELL by Robbi Sommers. 192 pp. Scorching stories
by the author of *Pleasures*.   ISBN 1-56280-005-1   10.95

STILL WATERS by Pat Welch. 208 pp. A Helen Black mystery.
2nd in a series.   ISBN 0-941483-97-5   9.95

These are just a few of the many Naiad Press titles — we are the oldest and
largest lesbian/feminist publishing company in the world. Please request a
complete catalog. We offer personal service; we encourage and welcome
direct mail orders from individuals who have limited access to bookstores
carrying our publications.